King Humpty Dumpty

A Pantomime

Paul Reakes

A Samuel French Acting Edition

FOUNDED 1830

SAMUELFRENCH-LONDON.CO.UK
SAMUELFRENCH.COM

Copyright © 2005 by Paul Reakes
All Rights Reserved

KING HUMPTY DUMPTY is fully protected under the copyright laws of the British Commonwealth, including Canada, the United States of America, and all other countries of the Copyright Union. All rights, including professional and amateur stage productions, recitation, lecturing, public reading, motion picture, radio broadcasting, television and the rights of translation into foreign languages are strictly reserved.

ISBN 978-0-573-16401-9

www.samuelfrench-london.co.uk

www.samuelfrench.com

FOR AMATEUR PRODUCTION ENQUIRIES

UNITED KINGDOM AND WORLD EXCLUDING NORTH AMERICA

plays@SamuelFrench-London.co.uk

020 7255 4302/01

Each title is subject to availability from Samuel French,

depending upon country of performance.

CAUTION: Professional and amateur producers are hereby warned that *KING HUMPTY DUMPTY* is subject to a licensing fee. Publication of this play does not imply availability for performance. Both amateurs and professionals considering a production are strongly advised to apply to the appropriate agent before starting rehearsals, advertising, or booking a theatre. A licensing fee must be paid whether the title is presented for charity or gain and whether or not admission is charged.

The professional rights in this play are controlled by Samuel French Ltd, 52 Fitzroy Street, London, W1T 5JR.

No one shall make any changes in this title for the purpose of production. No part of this book may be reproduced, stored in a retrieval system, or transmitted in any form, by any means, now known or yet to be invented, including mechanical, electronic, photocopying, recording, videotaping, or otherwise, without the prior written permission of the publisher. No one shall upload this title, or part of this title, to any social media websites.

The right of Paul Reakes to be identified as author of this work has been asserted by him in accordance with Section 77 of the Copyright, Designs and Patents Act 1988

CHARACTERS

Jinxit, the bad luck fairy
Humpty Dumpty
Good Fairy
Patsy Putumup, dame, landlady of the "Egg View" B&B
Captain Vince Valiant of the King's Men, principal boy
Private Spit
Private Polish
Horace, the horse
King
Queen
Princess Penelope
Fiona, her lady-in-waiting

Chorus of **Fairies**, **Holiday-makers**, **Children**, **King's Men**, **Footman**, **Head Cook**, **Courtiers** and **Cooks**

SYNOPSIS OF SCENES

ACT I

Scene 1　Domain of the Bad Luck Fairy
Scene 2　Eggton-On-Sea
Scene 3　On the Way to the Beach
Scene 4　The Beach at Eggton-On-Sea

ACT II

Scene 1　Domain of the Bad Luck Fairy
Scene 2　The Royal Palace
Scene 3　A Dungeon Cell
Scene 4　Eggton-On-Sea
Scene 5　A Spot of Yolk Singing
Scene 6　The Grand Finale

MUSICAL NUMBERS

Overture

ACT I

Song 1	Song and dance	Chorus and Dancers
Song 2	Comedy song	Patsy
Song 3	Song and dance	Captain, Chorus, Children and Dancers
Song 4	Song and dance	King, Penelope, Fiona, Captain and Chorus
Song 5	Song and dance	Patsy, Humpty, Chorus and Children
Song 6	Song and dance	Chorus and Dancers
Song 7	Romantic duet	Captain and Penelope
Song 8	Comedy song and dance	King, Patsy, Chorus and Dancers
Song 9	Song and dance	Humpty, Patsy, Chorus and Dancers

Entr'acte

ACT II

Song 10	Song and dance	Fiona, Chorus and Dancers
Song 11	Song	Fiona and Humpty
Song 12	Comedy song and dance	Patsy, Spit and Polish and Chorus
Song 13	Reprise of song 10	Fiona
Song 14	**(Optional)** Song and dance	Captain and Penelope
Song 15	Song and dance	Chorus and Children
Song 16	Song and dance	Company
Song 17	House song	Company
Song 18	Finale song or reprise	Company

A licence issued by Samuel French Ltd to perform this play does not include permission to use the Incidental music specified in this copy. Where the place of performance is already licensed by the PERFORMING RIGHT SOCIETY a return of the music used must be made to them. If the place of performance is not so licensed then application should be made to the PERFORMING RIGHT SOCIETY LTD, 29-33 Berners Street, London W1T 4AB.

A separate and additional licence from PHONOGRAPHIC PERFORMANCES LTD, 1 Upper James Street, London W1R 3HG is needed whenever commercial recordings are used.

CHARACTERS AND COSTUMES

Jinxit is the Bad Luck Fairy. She is a thoroughly nasty piece of work. The one we all love to hate. She never misses an opportunity of stirring the audience into a frenzy of boos and hisses. She can turn on the oily charm, especially in the scenes where she tries to get the mortals to break the egg for her. A strong personality is needed for this role. No singing or dancing ability is required and most of her dialogue is spoken in rhyme. She is very weird and uncanny in appearance, with bizarre hairdos, make-up and costumes to match. When searching for the egg, she disguises herself as a mortal, but she still appears grotesque and alarming. She disguises her magic wand as an oddly shaped umbrella.

Humpty Dumpty is about as appealing as rampant toothache! He is a cocky, obnoxious, uncouth youth who revels in being extremely unpleasant to everyone he meets, including the audience. When released from the egg, and having three magic wishes at his disposal, he is even more insufferable. However, under the influence of young Fiona he is made to see the error of his ways and eventually brings about a happy ending for all concerned. Ideally the part should be played by a teenage male. A confident performer is needed who will dominate the stage and give the audience as good as he gets. Some singing and dancing is called for, but strong acting ability is paramount. For Act I his costume should be a mixture of "Pantoland" and contemporary teenage street wear. For Act II he dons a sumptuous regal outfit. Finale costume.

The **Good Fairy** is the complete opposite of Jinxit. She is beautiful, charming and has a lovely speaking voice. She is always very polite and gracious, even when dealing with the loathsome Jinxit. To protect Humpty from the bad fairy's evil influence, she resolves to put him inside an enormous egg. She is also convinced that the wayward lad has a better side to his nature. No singing or dancing is required, but good poise and graceful movement is essential. All her dialogue is spoken in rhyme. She is radiant in her shining fairy costume and immaculate hairdo. She carries a magic wand, of course.

Patsy Putumup (Dame) is the landlady of a local B&B. She can be coarse, overbearing and fond of giving herself airs and graces. Lily Savage, Sybil Fawlty and Hyacinth Bucket all rolled into one! Whatever her faults, you can't help liking the old girl. She is on friendly and confidential terms with the audience and never misses an opportunity of involving them. When Humpty Dumpty uses his magic wish to make her his mother she dotes on him with sickening sentimentality. And later, when she is made Queen Mother, her delusions of grandeur go right through the roof. It goes without saying that all her costumes, hairdos and make-up are outrageous and funny. Apart from her everyday gear, she gets to wear a ludicrous bathing costume and cap and an array of ridiculous regal raiments and crowns. Speciality Finale costume.

Captain Vince Valiant of the King's Men (Principal boy). He is a handsome young officer, bold and dashing with the best legs in the regiment! He and Princess Penelope are secretly in love, but the difference in their social standing cause the usual problems that beset young lovers. However, through the unintentional help of Humpty Dumpty, their problems are solved and wedding-bells ring out. A charismatic personality with strong singing and dancing ability is required. His resplendent Captain's uniform is of the "Quality Street" variety. Plumed shako cap and a red tunic with gold epaulettes, belt and frogging. Knee boots with tight white leggings or fish nets. Magnificent Finale dress uniform.

Privates Spit and **Polish** of the King's Men. Why such an incompetent pair of military misfits should be allowed to remain in the King's Army is a complete and utter mystery! But we are glad they do, because they are such a likeable and funny duo. Spit tries to retain a certain military bearing, while Polish is just a bumbling, lovable nitwit. They are involved in plenty of audience participation and comic capers, especially with Horace the horse and Patsy Putumup. Singing and dancing ability is an advantage, but good comic timing and camaraderie with the audience is essential. Their uniforms are comically ill-fitting and ramshackle. Shako caps, red tunics with white belt and cross bands. White trousers with red or gold side stripes. Finale uniforms.

Horace, the horse is the regimental mascot. A frisky, four-legged friend who is cheeky, mischievous, and above all, lovable to the youngsters in the audience. He is involved in quite a lot of the action and musical numbers, so good team work under the skin is called for to make the most of this comical critter. A good "horse skin" is required with movable eyelids, tail, etc. It is advisable to have this well in use before the actual production. A small decorated straw hat or flowered garland for the Finale.

The **King** is a very affable old boy who treats everyone, including the audience, like long-lost friends. He is fun loving, full of bonhomie, has an eye for the ladies (even Patsy Putumup!), and generally takes life as it comes. Even being henpecked by the Queen, and eventually losing his crown to Humpty Dumpty, is accepted as part of life's rich tapestry. A charismatic personality with a good sense of comedy is required for this character part. Singing and dancing ability is a bonus. Apart from his Royal "walk about" attire and crown, he gets to wear an old-fashioned striped bathing costume and a shabby servant's outfit. Magnificent regal robes and crown for the Finale.

The **Queen** is the Queen, and let there be no doubt about it! She is a haughty, dominating battle-axe with absolutely no sense of humour or fun. You laugh at her and never with her. She bullies the King and is exasperated by his familiarity with the "riff raff". She is horrified to discover that her daughter loves a commoner. When Humpty takes over the throne, reducing her to a palace cleaner, her whole world collapses. A strong personality is required for this role. Singing and dancing ability a bonus. Like the King, she gets to wear royal "walk about" attire and crown, an old-fashioned bathing costume, and a shabby servant's outfit. Magnificent regal robes and crown for the Finale.

Princess Penelope (Principal Girl) is a beautiful and charming young lady, who shares her father's friendliness and affability with the common "riff raff". So much so, that she is secretly in love with one of them. When this is revealed, and Captain Valiant is banished from the Kingdom, she is naturally devastated. But that is not her only problem. Horrible Humpty wants her as his wife. She boldly defies him, even when he threatens to use his last magic wish to make her comply. A charming personality with strong singing and dancing ability is needed. Like her parents, she gets to wear splendid royal "walk about" attire, a very becoming bathing suit (this is optional), and a shabby servant's outfit. Magnificent regal robes and crown for the Finale.

Fiona is a lady-in-waiting to the Princess. She is a pretty, petite young woman, and should be compatible in age to Humpty Dumpty. For some peculiar reason she takes a liking to Humpty and falls for him in a big way. Well, somebody had to! Like the Good Fairy she also believes that there is a better side to his personality. Singing and dancing ability is required. Being a lady-in-waiting to royalty, she is always exquisitely dressed. A bathing suit for the beach scene is optional. Finale costume.

The **Chorus, Dancers** and **Children** appear as Fairies (large and small), Holiday-makers, King's Men, Courtiers and Junior Cooks. All participate in the action and most of the musical numbers, with costumes appropriate to their calling. The King's Men (Dancers) wear a smart version of the uniform worn by Spit and Polish. If it's an all-female dancing troupe, tights can be substituted for the white trousers. There are three cameo roles: a dignified Footman, a harassed Head Cook (male or female), and a shapely young female bather who appears in a very skimpy swimsuit! (One of the dancers.)

PRODUCTION NOTES

The pantomime offers opportunities for elaborate staging, but can be produced quite simply if funds and facilities are limited.

There are three full sets:
Eggton-On-Sea
The Beach at Eggton-On-Sea
The Royal Palace

These scenes are interlinked with tabs or front-cloth scenes:
Domain of the Bad Luck Fairy
On the Way to the Beach
A Dungeon Cell

There can be a special Finale setting or the Eggton-On-Sea full set can be used.

The Giant Egg

The actual size of your giant egg is entirely up to you. But it must be remembered (with artistic licence!) that Humpty Dumpty is supposed to be inside it. It can be a simple painted cut-out, but the more adventurous prop designers may like to try their hand at constructing a three dimensional giant egg. This would look far more effective. Two giant halves of broken eggshell are also required.

You may find it necessary to use two eggs because of the quick change between SCENES 1 and 2 of ACT I. Of course, if the same egg can be re-positioned easily for the opening of SCENE 2, no problem. For ACT I, SCENE 1 the egg should be mounted on a small trolley for mobility and support. Also, it will require some form of support when it is sitting on the wall. In ACT I, SCENE 2, when it is supposedly dropped and broken, the egg is removed during the black-out and the two halves of broken shell left on the ground in its place. The reverse of this happens in ACT II, SCENE 4, when Jinxit is put inside the egg and it's transported away by the Good Fairy. Here the small trolley can again be used for mobility and support.

Dancing in the Sea
A simple method is to have a series of tiered ground rows, cut and painted to represent stylized waves. These must be carefully spaced to enable your dancers to perform comfortably between them. You could, of course, try a method using lengths of blue and green material. The ends of these lengths are concealed off stage and gently wafted to create the effect of billowing waves. The dancers will give the impression of frolicking about in moving water. It will take some careful rehearsing to perfect, but the end result will be well worth it.

The Deckchair
The actual comic business is left to the individual director, but it must be a carefully thought out and well-rehearsed slapstick routine. It involves the antics of Patsy and Spit and Polish as they literally wrestle with the problems of trying to erect a very uncooperative deckchair. A hilarious tussle of tangled arms and legs, crushed fingers, trodden-on toes and trapped heads. To end the routine it would be effective to have the chair thrown aside in exasperation and miraculously land in the correct "set up" position, only to collapse again as Patsy sits on it.

Lighting and Effects
Nothing extraordinary is called for. There is the usual helping of flashes with puffs of smoke, eerie and magical sounds, rolls of thunder and flashes of lightning. There are several complete black-outs to enable the appearance and disappearance of the giant egg or characters. It goes without saying that these magical moments should be achieved as swiftly as possible before normal service is resumed! Extra use of lighting and follow-spots for musical numbers or appearances, etc., is left to the individual director.

Cuts
If you find your production is running too long please feel free to make cuts to the front-cloth scenes, for example Act I, Scene 3.

Paul Reakes

Other works by Paul Reakes
published by Samuel French Ltd

Pantomimes:

Babes in the Wood
Bluebeard
Dick Turpin
King Arthur
Little Jack Horner
Little Miss Muffet
Little Red Riding Hood
Little Tommy Tucker
Old Mother Hubbard
Robinson Crusoe and the Pirates
Santa in Space
Sinbad the Sailor

Plays:

Bang, You're Dead!
Mantrap

To Mary,
Who has looked after me so well
during the last thirty years.

ACT I

Scene 1

Overture

Domain of the Bad Luck Fairy

The CURTAIN *rises on a front-cloth showing a weird, surreal landscape. There are flashes of lightning and rolls of thunder, sinister lighting and unearthly sounds. Spooky music plays*

There is a flash DL

Jinxit, the repulsive Bad Luck Fairy, appears DL. *She sneers and snarls at the audience, provoking them into boos and hisses*

Jinxit Beware you puny mortals! Jinxit is my name!
I'm the Bad Luck Fairy! Causing havoc is my game!
All bad luck that comes your way,
Is caused by me I'm pleased to say!
When you go to a party to flirt with your dimples,
It's me who gives you those ugly great pimples!
If at Lotto you win, and you tell your boss to stick it,
It's me who loses your winning ticket!
When you visit the loo, I cut my best caper,
It's me who hides that last roll of paper!
For centuries past I have worked on my own,
But the job's got so vast I can't manage alone
So to ensure that bad luck remains consistent,
I have decided to take on a little assistant.
Humpty Dumpty is the name of the boy.
He's the young rascal I hope to employ.
(*She looks off* DL)
Ah! Here he comes! He's right on cue!
Let's greet the lad with a nice hiss and boo!

The audience are encouraged to comply

Humpty Dumpty, young and scowling, enters DL. *He sneers and jeers at the audience in return*

Humpty Yah! Boo yerselves! You rotten lot!
You don't scare me! You don't matter a jot!
You're just a bunch of [local] losers!
Dopey young kids and fat old boozers!
Jinxit Oh, he's just the lad to do the job!
He's such a nasty little yob!
Tell me, Humpty. Have you made a decision?
Will you accept this fine position?
Humpty Before I do — I wanna ask.
Wos the pay for doin' the task?
Jinxit *Three magic wishes* shall be your wage.
That's a good rate of pay for a boy your age.
Humpty Three magic wishes! Wow! That sounds great!
(*He offers his hand*)
Put it there! I'll be your mate!

They shake hands

Let's get to work! I can 'ardly wait,
To bring bad luck to those I hate!
(*He indicates the audience*)
Can I start wiv them?! They all need zappin'!
They're just an accident waitin' to 'appen!
Jinxit All in good time, my evil young poppet.
The fools of [nearby local place] are the next to cop it!
Come with me and I'll show you the ropes.
I'll teach you the way to annoy these dopes!

Cackling and sneering, they make their way towards the exit DL

There is a flash DR. *Suitable fairy music plays*

The beautiful Good Fairy appears DR

This halts Humpty and Jinxit in their tracks

Good Fairy Hold!
Humpty (*ogling the Good Fairy*) Cor! She's a tasty lookin' cracker!
Jinxit Don't be fooled! That hair's full of lacquer!
(*To the Good Fairy*) Get back on your Christmas tree!
Why are you here to bother me?

Act I, Scene 1

Good Fairy Can't you guess? (*Indicating the audience*) I bet they can!
(*To the audience*) I am here to foil her plan.
(*To Jinxit*) I will tell you the reason for this interruption.
I cannot allow this young boy's corruption.
He may be nasty and a bit of a whiner,
But for all his faults he is still a minor.
Jinxit He belongs to me! We've made a pact!
You can do nothing! And that's a fact!
Good Fairy What you are saying is quite untrue.
I have the power to protect him from you.
I know of a place, the ideal location,
Where he will be free from your contamination.
He will not like it. He will plead and beg.
I am going to put him — inside an egg!

Jinxit hoots with jeering laughter. Humpty shows unease

Jinxit Pay no heed to this witless wally!
She's clearly off her tinselled trolley!
Good Fairy (*raising her magic wand*) My fairy helpers, I summon thee!
Bring at once the egg to me!

The lighting becomes bright and magical. Fairy music plays

A band of small Fairies trip on and group themselves about the stage. Two larger Fairies enter, pushing on an enormous egg. (See Production Notes) They position it C

Humpty recoils in horror

Humpty (*appealing to Jinxit*) Don't just stand there!
Give her a kickin'!
She's gonna change me into a chicken!
Jinxit Now don't you worry, Humpty dear.
Her puny magic can't work here!

The Good Fairy turns towards the egg and raises her wand. Magical music plays

Good Fairy (*casting the magic spell*) I call upon the power of fairy magic,
To help me prevent this thing most tragic.

> I summon your aid in casting this spell,
> Put Humpty Dumpty inside this shell!
> (*She points her wand directly at Humpty*)

There is a blinding flash, followed by a complete black-out. Magical music continues

During the black-out, Humpty vanishes, presumably inside the egg

The Lights come up

(*To Jinxit*) Now he is safe from your vile pollution!
(*To the audience*) Believe me, folks, it was the only solution.
Jinxit (*enraged*) I will not be outdone by the likes of you!
Let's see what a little of my magic can do!
(*With a fiendish cackle, she raises her wand and prepares to cast her evil spell*)

The lighting becomes dark and sinister and spooky music plays under

> O Powers of Darkness and things most scary,
> Help me defeat this meddlesome Fairy!
> O Evil Powers, direct from hell,
> Crack this egg and shatter its shell!
> (*She points her wand at the egg*)

Nothing happens! Infuriated, Jinxit repeats the last two lines of her spell and points her wand. Again nothing happens. The Good Fairy's helpers giggle uncontrollably. The lighting becomes brighter and the music fades out

Good Fairy The egg is protected by my magic charm.
Your wicked powers can do it no harm.
Now only mortals can render it open.
Only by them can the eggshell be broken.
And as no mortals inhabit this domain,
Forever intact shall the egg remain.
Come, my Fairies, our work here is done.
Humpty Dumpty is safe from that evil one.

The Good Fairy exits DR, *followed by her band of Fairies*

Jinxit cackles to the audience

Jinxit That's where she's wrong! The dozy pimple!

Act I, Scene 2

> The way around this one is very simple.
> I will send the egg to where mortals dwell!
> To their dominion, I will dispatch this shell!
> *(Cackling, she raises her wand)*
> The powers of darkness I now invoke!
> Transport this egg and its precious yolk!
> Take it swiftly through the magic portals,
> And deposit it safely in the land of mortals!
> *(She waves her wand over the egg)*

There is a flash, followed by a complete black-out. Spooky music plays. During the black-out the egg vanishes. An eerie spotlight comes up on Jinxit and she roars with triumphant laughter

> Hee! Hee!
> See how easily her plans I foil!
> The egg now rests on mortal soil!
> Its exact location is not quite clear,
> But I'll seek it out, never you fear!
> With the help of some deluded mortal,
> Humpty will be set free! Chortle! Chortle!
> Once that egg is smashed to rubble,
> He will be free — to cause lots of trouble!
> Hee! Hee! Hee!!

With fiendish laughter and snarls at the audience, she sweeps out DL

The spotlight fades to black-out

Scene change music plays

Scene 2

Eggton-On-Sea. Many years later

A back-cloth shows the seaside resort with beach and pier, etc. Prominent R *is the front of Patsy Putumup's Bed and Breakfast establishment. It is gaudily painted and decorated with a profusion of shells, hanging baskets and window-boxes, etc. It has a practical front door and a hanging sign which reads "EGG VIEW B&B". A smaller sign hangs underneath reading "NO VACANCIES".* L *are houses and shops. Across the back runs a low wall. In the centre, on a thicker section of wall, sits Humpty's egg. (See Production Notes). Beneath the egg is a plaque which reads "THE GIANT EGG OF EGGTON-ON-SEA. DO NOT TOUCH". Near the back is a sign-post pointing off* L *marked "TO THE BEACH"*

When the Lights come up, the Chorus and Dancers, as holiday-makers, are discovered. They are equipped with the usual seaside holiday paraphernalia. They go straight into a lively opening song and dance

Song 1

After the number, a commotion is heard coming from the B&B

The B&B doors flies open and a Man comes hurtling out, landing on the ground. A second later the irate figure of Patsy Putumup follows him out, throwing the Man's suitcase after him

The Chorus look on in awe

Patsy OUT!! Out you go, and out you stay!
Man (*cowering on the ground*) But, I ——
Patsy Oh, I've 'ad your sort 'ere before! You're all the same! Never satisfied! This is the finest Bed and Breakfast establishment this side of [local place]! A proper palace, it is! But are you grateful? Oh, no! It's always the same! Nothin's right! It's moan, moan, MOAN!
Man But, I ——
Patsy Well, I can do without the likes of you! Go to the [local hotel], and see if they'll put up with yer snide remarks and incinerations! Go on! Clear off! Never darken my 'and towels again!

The Man scrabbles to his feet and makes for the exit L

(*Bellowing at him*) Scram!!

The Man runs out L

Patsy picks up his suitcase, moves L, *and throws it out after him. A yell of agony is heard. She dusts off her hands, then turns to the Chorus. She is now beaming with hospitality*

Ah! Good-morning, everyone! Good-morning! And may I say, what a lovely morning it is to be sure! Very bracing! Well, I now have a vacancy at my little B&B. Would anyone like to fill my gap?

The Chorus rush off in various directions

(*Calling after them*) You don't know what you're missin'! There's no bugs in my beds or soya in my sausages! (*To the audience*) I dunno! You just can't 'elp some folk, can ya?

Act I, Scene 2

The audience make a few replies

I said — (*loudly*) you just can't 'elp some folk, can ya?!

More response from the audience

That's better! I thought you'd dozed off for a minute. My name's Patsy Putumup, and I'm the landlady of that classy, up-market establishment over there. The Egg View B&B! Don't you think it's lovely? So tasteful and refeened. Not even [current *Changing Rooms* presenter] would spoil it! Are you lot stayin' 'ere on holiday?

Audience response of "No!"

Oh, just day-trippers. Where do you come from? (*Ad lib with various members of the audience*) Oh, I went there once, but it was shut! And you, luv? Where? ... Never 'eard of it! Is it somewhere in the land of the livin'? Anyway, you'll just love Eggton-On-Sea. It's worth comin' to just to see our main tourist attraction. (*Proudly pointing out the egg*) There it is! The Giant Hegg of Heggton-On-Sea! It's been sittin' on that wall for years an' years. No-one knows 'ow it got there or why. We just woke up one mornin', and there it was. And that's not the only thing on offer. There's a marvellous beach. And the front! (*She proudly thrusts out her chest*) I'll bet you've never seen such a fantastic front!

Audience reaction

Oh, you are awful! Just for that I'm gonna sing to you!

Song 2

A comedy song with audience participation if desired

(*To the audience*) Now, who'd like some accommodation? What about you, sir? Would you like me to put you up? Oh, I'd bend over backwards to fit you in! No? No takers? Suit yerselves! In that case, I'd better change the sign. (*She goes to the B&B and changes the sign to read "VACANCIES"*) It's no joke, y'know. A poor widow tryin' to run a place like this all on 'er own. (*Sadly*) 'Cos I am on me own, y'see. Completely and hutterly on me hown!

She encourages the audience to sigh for her

No! I'm more on me own than that!

The audience sigh again

Well, if you do change yer mind, don't be afraid to bang on my knockers at anytime. Bye for now!

She waves and exits into the B&B

The lighting becomes dark and sinister

Jinxit enters from L. She is disguised as a mortal, but there is still something weird and unsettling about her costume and appearance. Her magic wand is now transformed into a peculiar-looking umbrella. She greets the audience with snarls and sneers

Jinxit In this land of mortals I have searched far afield,
To find the egg in which Humpty Dumpty is sealed.
Many long years I've spent tracking it down,
And now I've arrived in this mouldy old town.
I have a strong feeling the egg is quite near!
Tell me, fools! Is it hiding around here?!

She by-plays with the audience, then she turns and sees the egg. Giving a triumphant cackle, she rushes up and speaks to it. An eerie follow-spot illuminates Jinxit and the egg

Listen, Humpty Dumpty! This is Jinxit! Remember me?!
After all these years of searching I am here to set you free.
But the egg is still protected by that meddling fairy's spell.
I will have to find a mortal who'll release you from its shell.
And remember, Humpty Dumpty, you are still my employee!
I gave you those three wishes, so your soul belongs to me!

She moves away from the egg to address the audience. The eerie spotlight continues to illuminate Jinxit

Now to find a mortal who will smash the egg in two!
That shouldn't be a problem, if they're all as dim as you!
(*She looks off* L)
Ah! Here comes some children! They're gullible and thick!
I'll get them to break the egg for me in less than half a tick!

Act I, Scene 2

Jinxit moves DR *and lurks*

The follow-spot fades and the lighting returns to the previous general lighting

A group of very bored Children enter L

1st Boy What a dump! Fancy bringing us here for a holiday!
1st Girl It's so boring! There's nothing to do!

The others agree. Jinxit moves over to them, with oily charm

Jinxit Good-morning, children. Why do you frown?
Aren't you content with the joys of this town?

The Children look at her and move away with suspicion

1st Boy (*to 1st Girl*) Who's she?
1st Girl I don't know, but someone should tell her that Hallowe'en is over!
Jinxit I assure you my intentions are very well meant.
I could not help noticing your sighs of discontent.
2nd Boy (*aside to others*) Why does she keep talking like Pam Ayres?
1st Girl (*to Jinxit; boldly*) Excuse me, but it's rather odd to go around talking in rhyme, you know.
Jinxit (*taken off guard*) Is that what I was doing, my little poppet?
(*Aside to the audience*) It might raise suspicion, so I'd better drop it.
(*To the Children*) You're quite right. I'm sorry. It's a bad habit I've got into. Do you really find this place boring?

They all confirm that they do

1st Boy Boring with a capital B! Once you've been on the beach there's nothing else to do here.
Jinxit Are there no places of interest or curiosities to see?
All Children Nothing!
Jinxit You amaze me. I would have thought a giant egg sitting on a wall was extremely interesting!

The Children turn and look at the egg

1st Boy (*uninterested*) Oh, that! That's boring too.
All Children Yeah! Boring!
Jinxit Aren't you in the least bit curious about it?

The Children move up and gather around the egg. Jinxit joins them

1st Girl It just says — (*reading the plaque*) "The Giant Egg of Eggton-On-Sea. Do not touch."
Jinxit Oh, I wouldn't take any notice of that, my dears. (*To one of the Boys*) Go on, young man! Why don't you give it a good hard push! Let's see what happens.
Boy Shall I?

With shouted encouragement from Jinxit and the Children, the Boy reaches out towards the egg and nearly touches it

Patsy comes out of the B&B. She sees what is happening and bellows

Her bellowing makes the Boy pull his hand away. Infuriated, Jinxit retreats into the background

The Chorus enter from various directions and take an interest in the proceedings

Patsy Oy!! Oy!! Oy!! Leave that egg alone!! (*She storms across, and points to the plaque*) Do-not-touch! (*To the Children*) Can't any of you lot read? Or do you go to [local school]?!
2nd Girl Why is there a giant egg sitting on the wall?
Patsy I don't know. But it's been sat sittin' on that wall for years an' years. Since time immoral.
1st Boy (*artfully*) I expect you can remember the day it was laid.
Patsy Well, I ... (*With a double take*) Watch it, you!
2nd Boy What sort of bird could lay a huge egg like that?
Patsy One with a very pained expression, I expect. Don't ask me! I'm not Bill Oddity!

Jinxit works her way to the front of the Chorus

Jinxit I imagine it would make a lovely big omelette! Enough to feed everyone here.

The Chorus and Children think this is a good idea

Or you could boil it. It would probably need more than three minutes though.

Again, they like the idea

Or you could fry it, poach it, scramble it or ——

Patsy Oy! that's enough from you, Delia! (*To All*) We'll 'ave no more talk of fryin', poachin', scramblin' or omelettin'! That egg stays intact! Nobody's gonna touch a hair on its 'ead. That's our main tourist attraction, that is. So! Leave that egg alone or you'll 'ave me to reckon with!

Patsy marches into the B&B

The Chorus talk amongst themselves. Jinxit, enraged, comes forward DS

Jinxit (*addressing the audience*)
Bah! My plan was foiled by that interfering old trout! I'll have to find another way to get young Humpty out!

Jinxit exits DR

The beat of a military drum is heard from off L

Women Hark! What's that?

The Children run and look off L

Children It's the King's Men!

The Children run back to join the others. Everyone looks excitedly towards L. *March music plays*

The handsome young Captain Vince Valiant marches on L, *leading the Dancers. They are all resplendent in the uniform of the King's Men. They march around the stage*

The Chorus cheer

The Captain halts C *and sings*

Song 3

If desired this can include the Chorus and Children. The song is followed by a military style dance routine for the Dancers. It ends with everyone saluting the audience

Captain (*calling the command*) Company! By the right! Quick march!

March music plays

The Captain leads the Dancers and they march out R. *The Chorus and Children follow them out, cheering and waving*

The march music continues

Private Spit and Private Polish march on L. *They wear comic versions of the military uniform and carry rifles. Their idea of marching is eccentric, to say the least! They do a lap of the stage. Spit comes to a sudden halt and Polish crashes into him and falls over*

Spit Halt!
Polish (*from the ground*) I wish you'd said that sooner! (*He gets up with comic business*)
Spit Where's the captain and the others gone?
Polish I dunno!

They both look about. Polish spots the audience and points to them

Let's ask them!
Spit (*seeing the audience for first time*) Oh! (*To them; waving*) Hallo!

"Hallo!" from the audience

We are the King's Men! I'm Private Spit! (*He steps forward smartly, stands to attention and salutes*)
Polish And I'm Private Polish! (*He does his own comic version of stepping forward, standing to attention and saluting*) We're looking for our spittoon.
Spit (*correcting him*) Platoon! You stupid boy!
Polish Yeah! 'Ave you seen 'em?
Spit You could hardly miss them. They were probably doing a lot of this ... (*He does a short comic version of the Dancers' routine*)
Polish 'An a lot of that! (*He does a comic camp version of the Dancers' routine*)
Spit Well? Have you seen them?

"Yes!" from the audience

Which way did they go?

The pair engage in business with the audience. The audience directs them the way they should go and the duo inevitably go the wrong way, etc. Eventually, they go R, *and look off*

Act I, Scene 2

Oh, there they are! Right at the other end of the street. With any luck the captain hasn't noticed we're missin'. We can ... (*Suddenly struck by a thought*) Hey! Aren't we forgetting something, you silly sentinel?
Polish Wot?
Spit Horace!
Polish Oh, Crikey!

They run around calling "Horace! Horace! Where are you? Horace!". Polish looks off L

Look! There he is!
Polish ⎫
Spit ⎭ (*calling; together*) Horace!! Come here!! At the double!

Music

Horace, the horse, trots on L. *He canters around the stage*

Spit and Polish go in pursuit of Horace. Eventually they catch him and bring him to the front

(*To the audience*) This is Horace! He's our regimental mascot!
Polish We used to have a goat, but it went and got a job with [local gag]! Say hallo to the nice people, Horace.

Horace bows to the audience

Spit He's very intelligent. Aren't you, Horace?

Horace nods

Watch this! What's two and two, Horace?

Horace taps out four with his foot. Spit and Polish encourage the audience to applaud. Horace curtsies

Polish Are you sure that's right, Horace? Doesn't two and two make six?
Horace (*shaking his head*) Neigh! Neigh!
Spit See! He's really clever! He must go to [local school]!
Polish And I bet he always comes top in — wait for it — the multiplication stables! (*He guffaws at his own joke*)

With comic business, Horace gives Polish a hefty push, knocking him over

During the comic business, Captain enters R, *and stands watching*

Seeing their Captain, Spit and Polish snap to attention and salute. Horace also stands at attention

Captain (*moving to them*) So! This is where you're hiding, is it?
Spit ⎫
Polish ⎬ (*calling*) Sah!
Captain Absent without leave, eh?
Spit Permission to speak, sah!
Captain Well?
Spit We got lost, sah!
Captain Lost?!
Spit ⎫
Polish ⎬ (*calling*) Y'sah!
Captain (*moving to Horace*) Is this true, Horace?

Horace nods

Did they get lost?

Horace nods

They didn't stop at [local shop] to buy you some carrots again, did they?
Horace (*shaking his head, emphatically*) Neigh!! Neigh!!
Captain (*moving back to the duo*) Well, it looks as though you're telling the truth. I'll let you off — this time.

Spit and Polish sigh with relief. Delighted, Horace frisks about

Patsy comes out of the B&B. She gets entangled with Horace!

Patsy Oi! Oi! Oi! What's all this?! What's goin' on 'ere?!
Captain (*moving over to Patsy; with a flashing smile*) Good-morning, ma'am. (*He salutes*) Captain Vince Valiant of the King's Men at your service! (*He gives her an elegant bow, then takes her hand and kisses it*)
Patsy (*overcome and wilting*) Oooooh! (*To the audience*) Oh, girls! What a little bobby dazzler! (*Moving back to the Captain*) What's 'appenin'? Is it one of them military taboos?
Captain No. This is Horace. Our regimental mascot. Say hallo, Horace.

With comic business, Horace nuzzles up to Patsy

Act I, Scene 2   15

Patsy (*pushing him away*) 'Ere! That's enough of the 'orse play! Keep yer 'ooves to yerself!
Captain (*to Horace*) Company mascot! Attention!

Horace springs to attention

> By the rights! Quick march! Left, right! Left, right! Pick 'em up! Pick 'em up!

Music plays

> *Horace marches out* L

Spit and Polish continue to stand at attention. Patsy goes over and peers curiously at them

Patsy Are these mascots as well?
Captain No. They're a couple of privates.

Patsy quickly glances at the audience

Patsy (*to Spit and Polish*) Yes ... Well ... There's no answer to that! (*She slinks back to the Captain*) Tell me, Captian. Are you on leave, or are you just about to go on — (*in a "sexy" voice*) manoooeuvres? (*She flutters her eyelashes at him*)
Captain Neither, ma'am. I am here to escort the royal party to the beach.
Patsy Oh! Are they back from their 'oliday then?
Captain Yes. The royal family returned last night. Their majesties will be here at any moment to take their annual swim in the sea.
Patsy (*getting excited*) Y'mean, they're comin' 'ere! The royals are gonna perambulate their precious posteriors past my palatial portals?!
Captain You can say that again.
Patsy Oh, no, I can't! Not without some more Poligrip! Oooh! I can't be seen in this old thing! I'd better go and get into me glad rags!

> *Patsy rushes into the B&B*

A fanfare is heard

Captain (*snapping to attention*) Men! Prepare to receive the royal party!

March music

Excitedly, the Chorus and Children rush on from all directions and fill the stage. The King's Men march on L and form ranks R

The Captain takes up his position in front of them. Spit and Polish take their places at the end of the line

The March music stops and another fanfare is heard. It is followed by grand processional music and cheers from the crowd

The King and Queen enter L. They are closely followed by the beautiful Princess Penelope. Lady Fiona, a pretty young lady-in-waiting, follows at a discreet distance. The Royals acknowledge the cheering crowd as they move DC. The King comes forward to speak to the conductor/pianist

King (*over the music*) Whoa! Whoa! That's enough! Don't blow a gasket! You're not down at the [local pub or club] now!

The grand music dwindles into silence. Princess Penelope and Fiona move into the crowd and during the following chat to them. The King spots the audience and waves to them

(*Calling out*) Oh, hallo there! Nice to see you all. Are you all right? Jolly Good! What do you think of it so far?

"Rubbish!" from the audience

Well, what did you expect? *The Lord of the Rings*! [Or topical gag]
Queen (*to the King; very displeased*) I do wish you wouldn't do that!
King Do what?
Queen Talk to all and sundry.
King Oh, is that their names! (*To the audience*) Hallo, Mr All! Hallo, Mrs Sundry! (*To the Queen*) It's all right. They don't mind.
Queen No, but I do! Where on earth is your decorum?
King Probably at home with the rest of my musical instruments! (*He laughs*)
Queen Oh, really!
King Come on. Lighten up, old girl.
Queen (*snapping at him*) Don't call me old girl!
King (*to the audience*) I know what I'd like to call her!
Queen What did you say?
King (*recoiling*) Er ... I said I'd like to be a bit taller.

Princess Penelope moves to her parents. Fiona follows her

Act I, Scene 2

Penelope What's going on?
Queen Nothing, Penelope, my dear. Your father is just being his usual disagreeable self.
King Me! You're the one standing there with a face like a bag full of spanners! She had a go at me, Penny, just because I spoke to the paying populace out there. (*He indicates the audience*)
Penelope (*looking out*) Oh! (*She waves to the audience*) Hallo! Hallo!
Queen (*annoyed*) Tch! Now you're doing it, Penelope!
Penelope Well, I thought that's what we royals were supposed to do. Wave and talk to people.
King Quite right, Penny. (*To the Queen*) You can't argue with that! (*To the audience*) What am I saying? She'd argue with Anne Robinson! And win! (*Moving to the Captain*) Ah, Captain Valiant! I trust everything has been hunky dory in our absence.
Captain Yes, your Majesty. I hope you had a pleasant holiday.
King (*confidentially*) Well, I did! Can't say the same for the old woman though. Still, I'd rather take her with me than kiss her goodbye.
Penelope We had a splendid holiday, Captain Valiant. Thank you for asking.
King I say! You appreciate a good song, don't you, Captain. We came across an absolute belter while we were on holiday, didn't we, Penny? Why don't we give everyone an earful of it?
Penelope (*embarrassed*) I — I don't think they'd be very interested.
Captain Indeed we would, your Highness. (*To the others*) Wouldn't we?
Chorus Yes!
Penelope Very well.

Song 4

A genteel, minuet style introduction is played as the King, Penelope and Fiona demurely bow and curtsy to each other, then step forward to sing. The music suddenly changes to loud rock and roll! The three belt the number out and gyrate around. The Captain and the delighted Chorus join in. Despite efforts from the King, the Queen refuses to take part. At the end, everyone cheers and applauds the King, Penelope and Fiona

> *During the applause, Patsy comes out of the B&B. She is now wearing an outrageously OTT outfit. It has a long train, which she has a lot of trouble with. She thinks the applause is for her and basks in it*

Patsy Oh, please! Please! There's no need to clap! I know I make [top model] look like [current scruffy personality], but there's really no need! (*To the audience*) Like it, girls? It's *Gap*! (*A double take*) I said *Gap*, young man! *Gap*! (*She struts about, showing off the outfit, and getting tangled up in her train. She spots the royals and rushes across*) Oh, your regalships! I do beg your royal puddin'!

Patsy attemps an elaborate curtsy but falls over. The King goes to her assistance, and they both get entangled in her train. Eventually they sort themselves out

King Good-morning. And you are?
Patsy Mrs Patsy Putumup, your imperial leather! (*Ultra posh*) Hi ham the proud proprietor of "Hegg View". The quaint little bed and breakfast hestablishment you see yonder.
King Are you doing a good trade?
Patsy Oh, yes! All season I've been full up! (*Proudly puffing out her chest*) Full to overflowing!
King (*reacting*) I see. It must be a huge asset as well.
Patsy Not really. It's just the way this dress hangs!
King I meant — being so near the seafront.
Patsy Oh, yes! Haw! Haw! Haw! Silly me! But I'm very concerned about our main tourist attraction.
King You mean the [local reference]?
Patsy No! The Giant Hegg of Heggton-On-Sea!

The Royals turn and look at the egg

Queen But it looks exactly the same as it always does! What's wrong with it?
Patsy Nothin' — yet! Listen!

Patsy brings the Royals further DS *and takes them into her confidence*

It's this new bunch of holiday-makers. I don't trust 'em. There was talk of scramblin', poachin' and omelette makin' earlier! If they break that egg, bang goes our tourist trade! And that will certainly be — wait for it — no yolk! (*To the audience*) See! I was right. It wasn't!
Queen The egg must be protected at all cost. (*To the King; sternly*) Do something about it!
King I will! (*To the audience*) I'd like to do something about her! (*Calling*) Captain Valiant!
Captain (*stepping up smartly and saluting*) Yes, your Majesty.
King You heard the old — er ... You heard the Queen. Make sure that no-one messes about with that jolly old egg of ours. Got that?
Captain Yes, your Majesty. I will see to it at once. Privates Spit and Polish!
Spit
Polish } (*together; stepping forward and saluting*) Y'sah!
Captain You will mount a twenty-four hour guard on the egg. On no account is anyone allowed to touch it. Understand?

Act I, Scene 2

Spit ⎫ (*together*)Y'sah!
Polish ⎭
Captain Carry on!

Spit and Polish shoulder their rifles, and march US *to the egg. Patsy follows them up. The duo stand to attention on either side of the egg. Note that it must be contrived that Polish is standing on the end of Patsy's train at this point, unseen by the audience*

Queen Now can we get on! I want to have my swim before the beach is crowded with commoners.
King Yes, we don't want you scaring too many people, my love! Lead on, Captain.
Captain (*saluting*) Yes, your Majesty. (*To the King's Men*) Royal escort! By the left! Quick march!

Music plays

> *The Captain leads the King's Men out* R. *The Royal party follow. The Chorus and Children exit after them, waving and cheering*

The music fades out

Patsy makes for the B&B, but pulls up with a jerk because Polish is standing on the end of her train. She makes another attempt and meets with the same obstruction. Finally, she gives her train a hefty tug, which causes Polish to fall over

Patsy (*to Polish*) That'll teach you to tamper with my tender behind!

> *Throwing the train over her shoulder, Patsy flounces into the B&B*

Spit Tch! Stuck out 'ere on guard duty for twenty-four hours! That means we're gonna miss *Richard and Judy*!
Polish And [TV Soap]!
Spit Come on! We'd better get on with it!

Spit and Polish march to and fro in front of the egg

> *Jinxit creeps on* DL. *She sees the guards and reacts in annoyance*

Jinxit (*addressing the audience*)
>Gr! Drat upon drat! The egg is under guard!
>To get it smashed now will be twice as hard!
>But wait! These soldiers have a mortal soul!
>I'll manipulate them to achieve my goal!
>(*She gives a cunning cackle, then moves up towards Spit and Polish*)

Spit and Polish challenge her, with rifles at the ready

Spit Halt! Who goes there?!
Polish Friend or foe?
Jinxit Friend.
Spit Advance friend and be recognized!

Jinxit goes nearer. They react at her bizarre appearance and back away

(*To Polish*) I don't recognize her! — I'm glad to say!
Polish (*peering*) I think I do! Wasn't she on "Buffy" last week?
Jinxit (*coming a little nearer; with her oily charm*) Good-morning. I am visiting the town on holiday. May I ask what you are doing?
Spit (*snapping to attention*) We are guarding the egg!
Polish (*snapping to attention*) For twenty-four hours!
Jinxit Twenty-four hours! Good gracious! That's an awfully long time to be standing outside. I'm afraid you're both going to get very wet.
Spit
Polish } (*relaxing; puzzled*) Wet?
Jinxit Yes. There's a terrible storm coming.

They look up at the sky, then back to her

Spit There's not a cloud in the sky.
Jinxit Look again!

Spit and Polish look up again. Unseen by them, Jinxit makes strange magical gestures with her wand, then points at the sky. There is a flash of lightning, followed by a roll of thunder. The lighting becomes dark and sinister. Spit and Polish react

Polish Crikey! Where did that come from?! (*To the audience*) She's better than [TV weather presenter]!
Spit Well, there's nothin' we can do about it. Whatever the weather we daren't leave our post!

Act I, Scene 2

Jinxit I have a suggestion to make. Why don't you move the egg to a place of shelter. That way you can still guard it while keeping warm and dry at the same time.
Polish (*to Spit*) 'Ere! Thas a good idea!
Spit (*unsure*) I — I don't know. (*To the audience*) Do you think we should move the egg, folks?

"No!" from the audience

Jinxit (*to the audience*) Oh, yes, they should!

The audience are encouraged into the "Oh, no, they shouldn't/ Oh, yes, they should!" routine with Jinxit

(*To the duo*) I think you'd better hurry up. It's going to pour down at any moment! (*Unseen by Spit and Polish, she points her wand at the sky*)

There is another flash of lightning and a roll of thunder. Spit and Polish react as before

Spit I know! Let's take it to the [local reference]. No-one ever goes in there.

Spit and Polish lean their rifles against the wall. Getting on each side of the egg, they gingerly lift it off the wall. It obviously heavy. They stagger DS, *carrying the egg between them. As they do so, Jinxit comes forward*

Jinxit (*addressing the audience, with devilish glee*)
>Just one little shock is all it will take,
>For these two fools the egg to break!
>For this they'll probably get a sacking!
>Here we go! It's time to get cracking!
>(*She makes magic gestures with her wand and points it at the sky*)

There is a blinding flash of lightning and a tremendous clap of thunder. Black-out. The sound of the egg falling and breaking is heard. There are cries of anguish from Spit and Polish, and triumphant laughter from Jinxit

Humpty Dumpty sits between two giant broken halves of eggshell lying on the ground

The Lights come up on Spit and Polish gaping at Humpty with mute amazement. Scowling, Humpty gets to his feet

Humpty (*confronting the awestruck pair*)What's up wiv you two? Shell shock?
Polish (*aghast*) Crikey! It's a talkin' chicken!

Spit and Polish panic, and run out R, *yelling "Captain! Captain!" at the top of their voices*

Jinxit	Hallo again, Humpty! You're looking very well,
	And none the worse for your time in that shell.
	I hope imprisonment has not made you mellow.
	I hope you are still an obnoxious young fellow.
Humpty	'Ave no fear, me evil old mate!
	I'm still the same chap, consumed with hate!
	I loathed that egg! Nowhere could I roam!
	But over the years it's become my 'ome.
	Those fools have reduced it to another Stone'enge!
	But with my magic wishes — I'll get my revenge!
Jinxit	That's my boy! That's music to my ears!
	Make them suffer and reduce them to tears!
	Treat them all with hate and scorn!
	Make 'em wish they'd never been born!

Jinxit sweeps out DL, *laughing evilly. Humpty turns to the audience and sneers at them*

Humpty   Oh, no! It's the [local] cretins again!
Which one of you is usin' the brain?
This talkin' in rhyme is gettin' a bore!
I've 'ad enough! I ain't doin' it no more!
You lot are a load of old rubbish! What are you?! Oh, yes, you are!

Humpty engages with the audience in the "Oh, no, we aren't/Oh, yes, you are!" routine

During the routine, the Captain, Spit and Polish and the Royal party rush on R. *The Chorus and Children rush on from all other entrances. Patsy comes out of the B&B. They all see Humpty, and start gabbling excitedly to each other*

Captain (*to all*) Silence!

They all go silent. Captain approaches Humpty, followed by Spit and Polish

Act I, Scene 2   23

Humpty Oh, look! It's the chocolate soldier and his two misshapes! (*He gives a mocking laugh*)
Captain (*to Spit and Polish*) Is this the thing that came out of the egg?
Spit ⎫
Polish ⎭ (*together*)Y'sah!
Humpty Oy! Not so much of — the thing! I've got a name! A name you'll all have cause to remember! (*Pompously*) I am Humpty Dumpty!

The Children laugh on hearing this. Humpty turns on the smallest girl

What are you laughin' at, droopy drawers?!
1st Boy (*squaring up to him*) You leave her alone!
Humpty An' what are you gonna do about it, Mr Muscle?

Humpty and the Boy nearly come to blows. The Captain strides across and gets between them

Captain Enough of this! (*To Humpty*) I'll thank you to keep a civil tongue in your head, young man. You are in the presence of royalty!

The King and Queen step forward and strike a regal pose. Humpty hoots with laughter

Humpty Get a load of them! Posh an' Becks eat yer 'eart out! (*He hoots with laughter again*)

There is general shock and indignation from the others, not least from the Queen

Queen Well! Really! This is disgraceful! (*To the King*) Don't just stand there! Reprimand this reprobate!
King Er ... Yes ... (*He moves to Humpty*) Now look here ... Rumpy Pumpy ... Or whatever your name is ... You mustn't be rude to my wife, y'know! Only I'm allowed to do that.
Humpty Your wife! Poor bloke! You must have been married durin' a total eclipse! (*He hoots with laughter*)

There are cries of outrage from the others and indignation from the Queen. Penelope moves to confront Humpty

Penelope Why are you being so rude to us? We haven't done you any harm.
Humpty (*giving her the once over and liking what he sees*) Cor! And who might you be, darlin'?

Captain Have some respect! This is Her Royal Highness, the Princess Penelope!
Humpty (*nudging Penelope*) Wotcha, Princess! Fancy a bag of chips later? Know wot I mean! Nudge, nudge! Wink, wink!
Captain (*grabbing Humpty by the arm*) I'm warning you! Any more of this disrespectful behaviour and I'll have you thrown into jail!
Humpty (*pulling away; angrily*) Just you try it, soldier boy, and see what 'appens! (*To the others*) And that goes for the rest of you dozy dummies!
Fiona If you dislike us so much, why don't you just leave?
Others (*in full agreement*) Yes!
Humpty Why should I?! It's your fault I'm 'ere in the first place!
King Our fault?
Humpty Yeah! (*Indicating Spit and Polish*) If those two clots hadn't smashed up my 'appy 'ome, I wouldn't be 'ere 'avin' to look at your ugly mugs! So! Wot you gonna do about it, your royal ridiculousness?
King Do?
Humpty I want my egg put back together again! (*He moves away and arrogantly folds his arms*)

The King gestures for the Captain to join him

King (*aside to the Captain*) We've got to get rid of this rude little rotter! (*Aloud*) What do you think, Captain? Can you repair the egg?

They inspect the broken pieces of shell

Captain (*shaking his head*) Impossible, I'd say, your Majesty. We're used to firing shells, not putting them back together.

Spit roars with laughter. As no-one else shares his mirth, the laughter soon dwindles into embarrassed silence

King Quite. (*He goes over to Humpty*) Well, Grumpy Dumpy! I'm afraid it can't be repaired. All the King's Horses and all Bob the Builder's men couldn't put your eggy back together again! Tell you what I'll do. I'll arrange for a taxi to take you to [next town or village], if you like?
Queen (*to Humpty; icily*) Yes! Go there! They're not very particular!
Humpty (*turning on them; viciously*) No way! I'm stayin' right 'ere! So! You can't repair my egg, eh! Well, I'm gonna have to use one of my three magic wishes to teach you a lesson!
Patsy Magic wishes! 'Ark at 'im! If you ask me, that egg's not the only thing that's cracked!

The others laugh. Fuming, Humpty strides over to Patsy

Act I, Scene 2

Humpty (*to Patsy*) You'll regret sayin' that, you ugly old trout!
Patsy (*outraged*) Ooh! I've never been so insulted in all my life!
Humpty Get away! With a face like that you must 'ave been!
Patsy (*fuming*) Oooh! If — If I was your mother I'd put you across my knee!
Humpty You could get a whole football team across one of your knees! So, you'd like to be my mother, would ya?
Patsy I would! I'd soon teach you some manners, young man!
Humpty Well, this is your lucky day!
        A son I will be just like no other!
        (*He points at Patsy*)
        I wish you were my dotin' mother!

The general lighting dims. Everyone, except Patsy and Humpty, freezes. A rosy spotlight shines on Patsy. Comic business as she appears to become strangely affected. The lighting returns to normal. The others unfreeze. Patsy becomes aware of Humpty, as if for the first time

Patsy (*overjoyed at the sight of him*) Oh, Humpty! My son! My little Humpty Wumpty!! Come to your mummy!
Humpty (*to the others, with triumphant disdain*) See!

Patsy rushes across and smothers the smug Humpty with hugs and kisses. General sensation as the others can't believe their eyes or ears. They look on with mouths agape

Patsy You're lookin' a bit off colour, sweetie pie! Is there anythin' Mummy can do for you?
Humpty Yeah! I'm starvin'! Get me some grub! Anything but eggs!
Patsy Certainly, my little cherub. Come along with Mummy and she'll soon fill up that empty tumsy wumsy of yours! (*She leads him towards the B&B*)
Humpty (*stopping*) Oy! Ain't you forgettin' somethin'?! (*He points to the pieces of eggshell*) My broken 'ome!
Patsy Of course, my little treasure.

Patsy picks up the pieces of eggshell and staggers into the B&B with them. Humpty follows her. Before entering the B&B, he turns to the gaping ensemble and gives them, and the audience, a gloating laugh, then exits

King Great suffering sceptres! Did you see that?! The little blighter was telling the truth! He does possess magic wishes!
Captain I think we need to be very wary of Master Humpty Dumpty, your Majesties. I have a feeling he could cause us a lot of trouble, if we're not careful.

Queen (*to King*) The captain is right. We don't want him using his magic wishes on us! So don't you go aggravating him!
Penelope All we have to do is keep out of his way. Don't have anything to do with him. With any luck he'll soon get tired of this place and go away.
Queen Let us hope so! And talking of going away, I still haven't had my swim yet! (*Snapping at the King*) Come along, do!

She sails out R

King (*to the audience*) She really isn't bad as wives go — The trouble is, she doesn't! Cheerio!

The King exits R, followed by Penelope, Fiona and Captain. Spit and Polish sneak out in the opposite direction. Humpty comes out of the B&B, eating a piece of cake. Patsy follows, fussing over him

Humpty (*munching the cake; addressing the audience*) Mmm! Mmm! This is smashin'! Mmm! Want some? Well, you can't! (*He crams the remainder of the cake into his mouth, gulps it down and laughs. With comic business, he wipes his sticky hands and mouth on Patsy's skirt*)
Patsy Are you sure you should 'ave eaten the whole cake, Humpty dear? We don't want you gettin' nasty collywobbles in oo's ickle tummsy wumsy!
Humpty It'll keep me goin' till lunchtime. I 'ope you don't begrudge me a little bit of cake, Mummy! (*He pretends to pout*)
Patsy (*throwing her arms around him*) Of course Mummy doesn't! Oh! There, there! Don't cry! Oh! Diddums!

Humpty is grinning at the audience over her shoulder

You can 'ave anythin' you want, my little sweetiekins! Your mummy'll give you whatever you ask for! I'll do anythin' for my little ray of sunshine! Anything!

Song 5

Song and dance for Patsy, Humpty, the Chorus and Children. It ends with Humpty standing C, in an arrogant pose, with Patsy looking at him with motherly pride and adoration

The Lights fade to black-out

Scene change music

Scene 3

On the Way to the Beach

The Lights come up on a front-cloth showing a pathway leading down to the sea and beach

The Lights dim and an eerie follow-spot comes up

Jinxit enters DL *into the follow-spot. She moves* C. *She is in a bad mood, and greets the audience with fiercer snarls than usual*

Jinxit Since being released from his prison of shell,
Young Humpty Dumpty is not doing very well!
He's wasted one wish on getting a mum!
He really deserves a kick up the bum!
I hope the fool doesn't waste the others!
I hope he's done with collecting mothers!
(*She turns away to* DL, *having a brooding sulk*)

The follow-spot fades and the general lighting becomes brighter

Spit and Polish enter DR

Polish Hey! Look! It's Peculiar Petulia! The one who made us break the egg. I'm gonna give her a piece of my mind!
Spit I'll do it! You need all the pieces you've got. (*He barks a command*) King's Men!

Spit and Polish move into single file with Spit leading

Advance!

They march across to Jinxit. She turns on them with a ferocious snarl

Advance back a bit!!

Jinxit advances on Spit and Polish, they back away, and are eventually flattened against the proscenium arch R

Jinxit What do you want, you dozy pair?!
I'm in a bad mood, so you'd better beware!
Spit (*timidly*) Y — You made us drop that egg ...

Polish Yeah! An' it got all broked!
Spit And now we're in trouble with our captain! We'll probably get court-martialled!
Polish And have our medals ripped off!

They both groan and grimace. This cheers Jinxit up, and she bursts into ghoulish laughter

Jinxit Hee! Hee! This really is the best of news!
It's helped to chase away my blues!
At least some misery you fools will taste.
Humpty's first wish has not gone to waste!

Laughing evilly, Jinxit sweeps out DL

Spit and Polish move C

Polish Ugh! She's 'orrible! (*To the audience*) Isn't she 'orrible, folks?

"Yes!" from the audience

Spit I reckon she's in cahoots with that Humpty Dumpty!
Polish Yeah! 'E's 'orrible too! (*To the audience*) Isn't 'e, folks?

"Yes!" from the audience

Spit And he's dangerous! With two magic wishes left, there's no telling what nasty things he'll get up to.
Polish Yeah! 'E might turn this whole place into [local/topical gag]!
Spit We'd better do as Princess Penelope said. Keep out of his way.
Polish You're right. (*To the audience*) Listen, folks. If you see that 'orrible Humpty Dumpty, you'll give us a shout, won't you?

"Yes!" from the audience

Spit
Polish } (*together*) Great! Thanks!

Unseen by Spit and Polish, Humpty enters DR. *He creeps up behind them*

The audience shout warnings

(*To the audience*) What's up? Is it him?

Act I, Scene 3

Spit (*to the audience*) Is he here now?
Polish (*looking to the sides*) I can't see 'im! Where is he?

"He's behind you!" from the audience

There is comic business with Spit and Polish turning around and Humpty keeping behind them. This is repeated a few times. Finally they come face to face with Humpty, yell and retreat to R, *where they cower together*

Humpty Well, well! If it isn't the buffoons of the butter fingers brigade! (*Viciously*) You two were responsible for breakin' my egg! I reckon you ought to be punished!
Polish (*scared*) Y-You're not g-gonna use one of your m-m-magic wishes on us, are you?!
Humpty (*with evil relish*) Yeah! That's jus' wot I am gonna do!
Spit
Polish } (*wailing and cringing; together*) Ooh, no!!
Humpty (*enjoying their misery*) Now, let me think! What excruciatin'—agonizin'—horrifyin' thing can I wish to 'appen to you two?
Spit
Polish } (*together*) Ooooow!!
Humpty Something that will really make you suffer!
Spit
Polish } (*together*) Ooooow!!
Humpty Something that will 'ave you beggin' for mercy!
Spit
Polish } (*together*) Ooooow!!
Humpty (*to the audience*) You got any ideas?

Humpty ad libs with the audience as they come up with suggestions

Spit (*to the audience*) Oy! I thought you lot were supposed to be on our side!
Humpty I know! I've thought of somethin' really nasty!
Spit
Polish } (*together, cowering in fright*) Oh, no!! Here it comes!!
Humpty (*turning to them; savouring every second*) I wish—I wish—Nah! I ain't gonna waste any of my wishes on you pair of plonkers! Get out!

Spit and Polish beat a very hasty exit DR

(*He turns to the audience*) I wouldn't mind usin' 'em on you lot though! (*Picking individuals from the audience*) I could turn you into a monkey! Oh, sorry! Someone's already done that! I could make you kiss that little girl next to you! I could make you [something topical/local]! I can do anythin' I like! With my magic wishes you're all in my power! Ha! Ha! Ha!

Patsy *(calling sweetly; off* DR*)* Humpty? Where are you, my little angel? Humpty?!

Humpty *(groaning)* Ugh! It's that old twit again! Silly old bat! Still, I can get anythin' I want out of her!

Patsy enters DR, *carrying a bulging supermarket bag. She rushes straight to Humpty and smothers him with hugs and kisses*

Patsy Oh, Humpty, my sweet! There you are! Silly old Mummy thought you'd run away and left her! Are you all right, my little snoockums?

Humpty I'm 'ungry!

Patsy I thought you might be, precious. Mummy's brought lots of yummy things. *(She opens the bag to show him the contents)* Now, what would you like to eat first?

Humpty *(snatching the bag)* The lot! *(He takes something from the bag and starts eating it greedily)*

Patsy *(to the audience)* Well, 'e's a growin' lad! *(To Humpty)* Humpty, dear, Mummy's got a special treat for her little lambkins. I thought we'd spend a lovely morning on the beach together. Enjoyin' the sun an' 'avin' a little paddle-waddle in the sea. What do you think of that, sweetie pie?

Humpty It stinks!!

Patsy Only when the wind is in the wrong direction.

Humpty Nah! Stoopid! I mean the whole idea stinks! I don't wanna go to no rotten, smelly beach!

Patsy Oh, but you'll like it, my little dove. Besides, the royal family are going to be there!

Humpty *(with interest)* That Princess Penelope?

Patsy Yes.

Humpty *(to the audience)* Cor! I really fancy 'er! *(To Patsy; aggressively)* Come on then! Wot ya waitin' for? Let's get to the beach!

Still eating, Humpty exits DL

Patsy watches him go, adoringly

Patsy *(to the audience)* Ah! Isn't he sweet?! Couldn't you just eat him up?! I bet you wish you had a son like my Humpty, don't you?

"No!" from the audience

Why not? 'E's a little darlin'! An angel! I know what it is! You're all jealous of me because I'm his mummy! Oh, yes, you are!

Act I, Scene 4

"Oh, no, we aren't!/Oh, yes, you are!" routine with the audience

Well, I can't stand 'ere arguin' with you lot! My little cherub needs his mummy! (*Calling to* DL) Comin', Humpty! Your mummy's comin'!

The Lights begin to fade

Patsy runs out DL

Black-out

Scene change music

Scene 4

The Beach at Eggton-On-Sea

There is a sea and sky back-cloth. On the ground are rows of stylized waves, or alternative effect. UL *is a brightly painted beach hut.* UR, *is a much grander beach hut bearing the royal crest. It has a curtained opening and a sign reading "KEEP OUT! NO RIFF-RAFF ALLOWED". There are tall rocks and sand dunes at the sides. There are a few low rocks for sitting and standing on*

The Chorus, Children and Dancers, all attired for the beach, are discovered. Enjoying themselves either lying in the bright blazing sunshine, playing games, eating ice-creams, making sand-castles or paddling in the sea, etc.

Song 6

During the song, the Chorus move to the sides and watch the Dancers as they leap among the waves and go into a dance routine. (See Production Notes) The whole number ends with a tableau

Horace trots on L, *and canters around the beach. This greatly amuses the children and annoys most of the adults*

Dragging the reluctant children with them, the Chorus and Dancers exit in all directions

Horace notices the larger hut and goes up to inspect it. He pushes his head through the opening in the curtain

Queen (*piercing scream; off from inside the larger hut*) Ahhhhgh!!

Horace hastily withdraws his head and trots out L

King (*off*) What's wrong now?
Queen (*off*) It was a horse! There's a horse out there!!
King (*off*) Oh! Get out of the way! Let me see!

The King emerges through the curtain. He wears his crown and a Victorian-style striped bathing costume with royal motif

(*To himself as he looks about the deserted beach*) Horse? What horse? I can't see any horse! Not even a seahorse! The old girl's gone potty! (*He spots the audience*) Oh, hallo again! Come to enjoy the beach as well, have you? Jolly good show! It's a lovely little spot with some outstanding views.

A very shapely female bather, clad in a skimpy one-piece swimming costume, enters L

(*He ogles the girl; to the audience*) And that's two of 'em!

The bather walks across in front of the King, turns to give him a saucy wave, then exits R

(*Gazing after her*) Absolutely breathtaking!

The Queen comes out of the hut. She too wears her crown and a Victorian-style bathing costume. She moves down into the King's line of vision

The King reacts, then tries to look past her R

Queen Have you seen it off?
King (*still looking to off* R) Not yet. D'you think she'd let me?
Queen I'm talking about the horse! The horse! The horse!
King The hoarse what? Oh, the horse! No. There isn't any horse.

Unseen by them, Horace trots on UL, *and goes straight into the royal hut*

Queen I tell you I saw a horse! It was here! I saw it!
King Sure it wasn't a pink elephant? You've been over doing that sun tan lotion, my love. You're supposed to rub the stuff in not drink it! (*He laughs*)
Queen (*infuriated*) Huh! You're impossible!

The Queen stomps into the hut

Act I, Scene 4

The King looks to off R. There is an ominous pause. The Queen gives a piercing scream from offstage. Horace neighs, off

Screaming, the Queen rushes out of the hut and runs off R

Horace comes out with a large brassière draped over his head

King *(moving to Horace)* Sorry if she gave you a fright, old fella. *(He sees the bra)* I say!! Love the water wings!

The King exits R

Spit and Polish run on L, out of breath

Spit *(seeing Horace)* There he is! *(They go over to Horace and see the bra)* Horace! Where did you get this?
Polish *(taking the bra)* Let's see! *(He stretches it out)* There's a label! *(Reading)* "HRH". Wos that mean? *(He stretches the bra again)* Oh, I know! Huge — round —
Spit Wait! That belongs to the Queen!
Spit ⎫
Polish ⎭ *(together; to Horace with shock)* Horace! You naughty boy!

Horace gives a whinnying laugh and gallops out R

Spit and Polish start to run after him

The Captain, Penelope and Fiona enter L. If desired, the two girls can wear attractive beach wear

Captain Halt!

Spit and Polish skid to a halt, snap to attention and salute. Unfortunately, Polish is still holding the bra and it hangs down over his face. Penelope and Fiona start giggling. The Captain, suppressing his own mirth, strides over to Spit and Polish

What's this? A new form of camouflage? Stand easy!

Spit and Polish obey the command, and Polish hides the bra behind his back

Now, you two. I want a full explanation of what happened to the egg. Why did you remove it from the wall, and how did it get broken?

Spit It was goin' to rain, sah. That weird lookin' woman said so, sah!
Polish There was lunder and thightning, sah!
Captain (*shaking his head in disbelief*) Weird looking woman! Thunder and lighting! That's a pretty lame excuse, even for you two! Let's have the truth. You were fooling around and knocked the egg off the wall, isn't that it?
Spit }
Polish } (*together*) No, sah!
Captain I'm going to put you both on a charge for this!

Penelope and Fiona move over to the Captain

Penelope Captain. Don't be too hard on them. Who knows what influence that awful Humpty Dumpty may have had on their actions. I'm sure they're not completely to blame for what happened.
Captain (*mulling this over*) Mmm ... Perhaps you are right, your Highness. (*To the duo*) Very well! On the advice of the princess, I'm giving you the benefit of the doubt. Now, be about your duties. Dismiss!

Spit and Polish snap to attention and salute. Once more, the bra obscures Polish's face. They march out R. Unseen, Humpty appears from behind the rocks, L. He crouches to watch and listen

Penelope My, how hot it is today.
Captain Indeed it is, your Highness. Perhaps Lady Fiona would be good enough to purchase some ice-cream.
Penelope What a splendid idea, Captain. (*To Fiona*) Would you oblige?
Fiona Certainly, your Highness. At once.

With a quick curtsy, Fiona exits L

Thinking they are now alone, the Captain and Penelope rush into each other's arms and embrace

Captain My darling!
Penelope My dearest!
Penelope Oh, Vince ... (*Looking about; scared*) Are you sure it's safe?
Captain Quite safe. We're completely alone.
Penelope I wish we could always be alone. Just you and I — alone together.
Captain It's a beautiful dream, my love. But alas, it can only be a dream. You're a royal princess and I'm just a common soldier.
Penelope That doesn't alter the fact that we love each other.
Captain True. But it does mean we can never be together.

Act I, Scene 4

Penelope (*tearfully burying her face in his chest*) Oh, Vince!

Humpty makes sick-making gestures, and disappears from view

Captain (*lifting Penelope's face*) Come, my darling. We mustn't let it spoil the few brief moments we do have alone together. Moments like this.

Song 7

A romantic duet and dance with romantic lighting. The number ends with the lovers embracing. The lighting returns to normal

Fiona enters L with three ice-cream cones

The lovers part quickly. Fiona hands out the ice-creams

Princess Penelope and Fiona exit L. The Captain watches them go, sighs to the audience, then exits R, mournfully licking his ice-cream

Humpty emerges from behind rocks L

Humpty (*to the audience; with disgust*) Yuk! What a soppy, sick-makin' scene that was! So! Princess Penny and the military moron are secretly in love, eh! I'll soon put a stop to that! 'Cos I fancy 'er meself. I wouldn't mind marryin' into royalty. And with my magic wishes I can do anythin' I like! Oh, yes I can!
Patsy (*off R, calling*) Yoohoo! Humpty! Where are you, my little sugarplum?

Patsy enters R. She wears a ludicrous frilly bathing costume and cap. She carries a folded deckchair

Oh, there you are, my little blossom! (*She drops the deckchair and rushes to hug and kiss Humpty*) Has Mummy's favourite little boy been for a nice paddle in the sea yet?
Humpty No! An' I don't want to neither!
Patsy Mummy's goin' to take a little dip later on.
Humpty That'll be nice for the fish! (*To the audience*) They'll think Moby Dick's come back!
Patsy (*to the audience; with a merry laugh*) Oh, he does like 'is little joke! (*To Humpty*) Well, what would you like to do, my cherub? Shall we make a sweet little sand-castle?
Humpty (*with disgust*) Do me a favour!
Patsy Does Mummy's little man want to sit in the sun and eat a nice big ice-cream?

Humpty Yeah! Make it two!
Patsy Oh! One for Mummy?
Humpty No! Both for baby!
Patsy All right, sweetie pie. 'Ere's some money. (*She delves into her bathing costume with lots of comic contortions to find a wad of banknotes. She gives some notes to Humpty*)

Humpty holds his hand out for the rest

Now, you go and buy as many ice-creams as you like, snookums. Mummy will put up the deckchair for you to rest your rosy little botty on when you come back. (*She turns away to pick up the deckchair*)

Humpty makes a face at her, then exits L *gloating over the money*

Patsy tries to erect the stubborn deckchair with lots of comic business

Spit and Polish enter

Spit and Polish see Patsy's predicament, and rush to her assistance. This only adds to the confusion, and very soon all three get into a hopeless tangle with the chair. (See Production Notes) Finally, more by accident than design, the chair is set up. Patsy goes to test it out and it collapses under her. The duo help her up with comic business

Ooh! Take the thing away! Take it away!

Spit and Polish exit R *with the chair*

I'll never shop at [local shop/store] again! (*Rubbing her painful posterior*) Ooooh!! I'm sure I've done meself a mischief! I'm gonna claim constipation for this, you see if I don't! Oh dear! What's my little Humpty gonna sit on now!

The King enters R. *The Chorus, Children and Dancers drift on from various directions carrying beach balls*

King Ah! Mrs Putumup!
Patsy What?! ... Oh! Your royal jelly! (*She does an awkward curtsy*) I didn't recognize you! I must say you look very comfy an' cosy in yer cossie.
King Not bad is it? It shows off the old figure a treat. (*He poses in profile, showing off his paunch*) I'm told that [TV/film heartthrob] has got one just like it!

Act I, Scene 4   37

Patsy (*to the audience; pointing to his belly*) So 'as John Prescott!
King Yours is very becoming too, Mrs Putumup
Patsy (*preening herself*) Oh, thank you, your royal flush! It's just a little thing I picked up locally.
King Ah! So that's what happened to the [local gag] tent! (*He laughs*)

Patsy feels obliged to join in

I hope you don't mind my little quip?
Patsy I didn't know it was showin'!

They both laugh

Oh, you mustn't let me carry on like this, Maj! You'll think I've got no proper respect for royalty.
King Nonsense! We all look the same in our bathing suits. That's what's so marvellous about being at the seaside!

Song 8

A jolly song and dance for the King, Patsy, Chorus and Dancers. The dance involves the use of beach balls. The number ends with Patsy and the King together in a comical pose, holding up two beach balls

The Queen enters R and sees Patsy and the King. She is followed by the Captain, Spit and Polish. Penelope and Fiona enter, L

Queen (*outraged*) What is the meaning of this?!

Patsy and the King topple against each other

King (*to the Queen; disentangling himself from Patsy*) Ah! There you are, my love! I was just ... er ... demonstrating some of those games we saw on our holiday.
Patsy Yes! 'E was showin' me how he can keep two balls in the air at the same time.
Queen (*icily*) I see! Come along! It is time we returned to the palace for luncheon!

Humpty strolls on, L, eating a large ice-cream cone. He sees the Royal pair's costumes and hoots with laughter

Humpty Cor! Get a load o' that! It's bananas in pyjamas!

Queen Huh! It's that awful uncouth youth again! (*To Patsy*) Now that you're his mother, I thought you are going to teach him some manners!
Patsy Yes ... Now, now, Humpty. You mustn't be rude to the royals.
Humpty Yah! Put a sock in it, you silly old moo! (*He sticks the ice-cream cone on her nose*)
Queen (*to Patsy; sarcastically*) I can see that you have perfect parental control.
Humpty (*to the Queen*) Ha! You're no great shacks at bein' a mother yerself! You don't know what your darlin' daughter's bin gettin' up too!

A general reaction from everyone, not least from the Captain and Penelope

Queen What on earth are you talking about?
Humpty Ask 'er! Go on! Ask 'er about the toy soldier over there!
Queen Penelope, come here!

Penelope crosses to the Queen

What is he saying?
Penelope I — I have no idea, Mama.
Humpty Oh, yes, she 'as! She and Captain Scarlet are secretly in love!

General reaction from the others

I saw 'em together meself! Being all luvvie duvvie! (*He mimics the lovers from earlier*) Oh, my darlin'! Oh, my dearest! You should 'ave seen 'em! [Current romantic couple in news] 'ave got nothin' on them two!
Queen (*shocked and staggered*) Penelope! Is this true? Answer me!
Penelope Yes! Yes, it is true! There I've said it! (*Proudly*) Captain Valiant and I do love each other!

Sensation! The Queen is staggered. The Captain, under his military bearing, looks very pleased and proud

Queen (*rounding on the King*) This is all your fault!
King (*to the audience*) I had a feeling it might be!
Queen Allowing her to consort with commoners! Well, don't just stand there! Do something!!
King Er ... Yes ... Er ... Captain Valiant — a word.
Captain (*marching over and saluting*) Yes, your Majesty.
King Do you love my daughter?
Captain (*proudly*) I do, your Majesty! With all my heart! (*He slaps his thigh*)

Act I, Scene 4   39

King Nicely done. (*To the Queen*) He seems awfully sincere.
Queen I don't care what he seems! It must be stopped immediately! We cannot allow our only daughter, a royal princess, to be in love with a common soldier! You will banish him at once from our kingdom!

General sensation! The two lovers are obviously greatly affected. Humpty hoots with laughter

King I say! Isn't that going a bit too far? Couldn't we just send him to [local place]?
Queen (*roaring at him*) Do as I say! Banish him!
King (*recoiling*) Ah! ... Yes (*To the Captain; formally*) Captain Valiant, I banish you from our kingdom! You return under pain of death! (*Informal aside to the Captain*) Sorry about this, old boy.
Penelope (*desperately*) No!
Queen Be silent, Penelope! (*To the Captain; pointing to* R) Go!

With tremendous control and dignity, the Captain salutes and marches out R

Humpty hoots with laughter. Princess Penelope tries to run after the Captain

Penelope (*desperately*) Vince! ...
Queen (*stopping her with raised hand*) Penelope!

Bursting into tears, Penelope is comforted by Fiona

Patsy (*aside to the audience*) What a carry on! Better than [TV soap] in'it?!
Humpty (*moving to Penelope*) Never mind, darlin'. Plenty more fish in the sea. 'Ow about yours truly? Why not let me show you a good time.
Penelope (*turning on him; angrily*) Get away from me! You ... You repulsive little sneak!
Humpty (*with mock shock*) Oh! Come, come! That's no way to talk to your fiancé!

General reaction!

Penelope (*unable to believe her own ears*) Fiancé?!
Humpty (*smugly*) Yeah! I've decided to marry you meself, Pen. (*To the King and Queen*) You are now lookin' at your future son-in-law! (*He hoots with laughter*)
Queen (*almost speechless*) I ... I ... (*Rounding on the King*) Do something!!
King (*going to Humpty*) Now look here, Lumpy Bumpy. This isn't on, y'know! It's simply not done!

Humpty Who says so?
King Well, I do. I'm her father, and I'm the king! (*He points to his crown*)
Humpty Not fer much longer!
                    To this land a change I'll bring!
                    I wish I was your ruling king!!

There is a flash, followed by a complete black-out. Magical music plays. When the lighting returns to normal, Humpty is wearing the King's crown. He stands C, with his hands on his hips, roaring with arrogant laughter. The others gape at him in mute amazement. The King reaches up to feel his now bare head. Still laughing, Humpty struts up and down, showing off the crown

    Long live the new king! (*He puts the crown at a rakish angle*) King Humpty Dumpty! (*To the others*) On yer knees, peasants!

They are still too dumbstruck to move

    (*Snarling at them*) Kneel.

They all kneel

    Rise!

They all stand

    (*He revels in his new found power*) Kneel!

They kneel

    Rise!

They stand

    Kneel!

They kneel

    Rise!

They wearily stand. He laughs, then turns his attention to the audience

    Oy! Why aren't you lot risin' an' kneelin'?! I'm the king now! You'll all do as I say from now on!

Act I, Scene 4   41

Patsy (*moving to Humpty; tentatively*) Humpty, my sweetness ...
Humpty (*arrogantly*) That's no way to address your king!
Patsy Sorry — your royal icing! (*She curtsies to him*) Does this mean I'm now a — a Queen Mummy?
Humpty Yeah! I 'spose it does! 'Ere! (*He whips off the Queen's crown and tosses it to Patsy*) Cop this!
Patsy (*putting the crown on*) Oooo! Lovely! (*She parades up and down; then to the audience*) Does my head look big in this?
Queen (*finding her voice at last; to the King*) Well! Aren't you going to do something?!
King What can I do? He's the king now!
Humpty (*to the Queen*) Yeah! And don't you forget it, face ache! (*To the others*) Don't any of you forget it!
King But what's to become of us? We've always been royals!
Humpty Well, you're commoners now!
Queen (*horrified*) Oooh!!
Humpty You'll 'ave to get a proper job!
King A *job*!!
Queen A *job*!!
Humpty Tell you what! I'll give you both jobs at my palace. As cleaners!
Queen (*horrified and disgusted*) Cleaners!!
Patsy (*to the Queen*) Yea verily! Thou art now an old scrubber! Get thee hence to yon palace and get thy finger out! Be gone from our royal presence! (*To the audience*) Ooh! I'm proper power mad!

The King leads the devastated Queen out R

Humpty hoots with laughter. Penelope moves to confront him

Penelope (*scornfully*) And what about me, your Majesty? Do I apply for a job at [local firm/shop]?!
Humpty Not necessary, darlin'. I want you to be my queen! Jus' say the word, an' we'll nip down to [local church/vicar] an' get 'itched right away.
Penelope Never! I will never marry you!
Humpty Oh, I think you will. Remember, I've still got one magic wish left. I could use it to make you my wife if I wanted to!
Penelope You wouldn't dare!
Humpty I can dare any thin'! I'm King Humpty Dumpty! (*He roars with laughter*)

Fuming and upset, Penelope runs out, L *followed by Fiona*

The Chorus look downcast

(*Looking around at the Chorus*) Wos the matter with you miserable lot?! This is my coronation day! Let's celebrate! Let's 'ave a knees up! Enjoy yerselves! That's a royal command! Enjoy yerselves — or else! (*To the Pianist/Conductor*) Come on, you! PLAY!!

Song 9

Humpty and Patsy sing and dance. After threats from Humpty, the Chorus and Dancers participate. Despite the situation, it turns into a lively number. As the Chorus and Dancers take over the singing and dancing, Humpty and Patsy stand on a rock to one side, and grandly survey their minions. The number ends with a big finish

The Music continues as the entire Chorus turn towards Humpty. He points downwards, and they all kneel and bow their heads. Humpty roars with triumphant laughter, and Patsy gives the audience the royal wave

The CURTAIN *falls*

Entr'acte

ACT II

Scene 1

Domain of the Bad Luck Fairy

The CURTAIN *rises on the front-cloth showing a weird, surreal landscape. The lighting is dark and sinister. There is a flash of lightning and a roll of thunder*

Jinxit enters DL, *laughing evilly. She goads the audience into boos and hisses*

Jinxit Young Humpty Dumpty is making good!
He's causing mischief as I knew he would!
To make himself king was a master stroke.
He now has power over these wretched folk!
The ex-princess lives in fear of her life.
Will he use his wish to make her his wife?
Her mother and father are made to grovel
They work like slaves and live in a hovel!
In all these miseries I can now revel,
Thanks to Humpty! That wicked young devil!!
(*Demoniacal laughter*) Ha! Ha! Ha!

There is a flash DR

The Good Fairy appears

The general lighting becomes brighter

        You've come too late! Your egg lies in rubble!
        Humpty is free, and he's causing lots of trouble!
Good Fairy I know all that. I've been following the plot.
Jinxit (*indicating the audience*)
        Which is more than can be said for that dozy lot!
Good Fairy One wish he used to gain a mother.
        To make himself king, he used another.
        One wish remains. There's a chance it might,
        Be used by Humpty to put all things to right.
Jinxit You must be joking, you deluded fairy!
        He's saving that wish for something really scary!

Good Fairy   You think he's as warped and evil as you.
On the surface he's vile, that's perfectly true,
But I firmly believe he is not thoroughly bad.
Deep down inside he's a decent young lad.
Jinxit (*roaring with laughter*) Ha! Ha! Ha!
You've got it all wrong! You don't know the score!
He's just like me! He's rotten to the core!
Just stick around and you will see,
The extent of that boy's devilry!
Hee! Hee! Hee!

Jinxit sweeps out DL, *laughing*

Good Fairy   (*to the audience*) You may agree with what she says,
That Humpty cannot mend his ways.
But I maintain he's not all bad.
It's just an irritating fad.
He's going through that awkward stage,
Of adolescent hate and rage.
It may take time, and things may worsen,
Before Humpty becomes a better person.
But happen it will, believe you me.
Meanwhile, let's follow his life of infamy.
(*She waves her wand*)

There is a flash, followed by a complete black-out

Scene 2

The Royal Palace

A sumptuous interior with pillars, chandeliers and rich draperies, etc. At the back are two tall windows overlooking the palace gardens. Between the windows there is a canopied dais with steps. On the dais, side by side, are two large golden thrones. The dais and steps are littered with empty food cartons, sweet wrappers and empty drinks cans, etc. There are entrances R *and* L

The music starts and the Lights come up. Humpty is discovered lounging on one of the thrones with his feet up on the other. He is eating a large slice of pizza. He wears the crown, and is attired in a magnificent regal costume. A dignified Footman, in white wig and livery, stands to one side of Humpty, holding an open pizza box. Fiona is discovered with the Chorus and Dancers. They are now elegant courtiers

Act II, Scene 2

Song 10

A song and dance number for Fiona, Chorus and Dancers to perfrom to their new monarch. (During the number, a speciality act can be introduced if desired.) Humpty is more interested in eating, and takes little, if any, notice of the proceedings. At the end of the number, the Chorus turn US with some trepidation. They bow and curtsy to Humpty

Humpty (*pretending to be pleased with their efforts*) Thank you. That was very nice indeed.

The Chorus show their obvious relief

(*Sitting up; his old malicious self*) If you like listenin' to a lot of parrots squawkin', or watchin' a herd of elephants clumpin' about! (*He stands up, and throws his pizza crust to the Footman*) That was the biggest load of rubbish I've ever seen! Absolute rubbish! (*He comes down from the dais*)

The Chorus hastily retreat to the sides

Call that singin' an' dancin'! It was lousy! I've seen better on *Pop Idol*!! [Or some other TV reference] (*To the audience*) They're complete and utter rubbish! Aren't they?

"No" from the audience

Oh, yes, they are!

"Oh, no, they aren't!"/ "Oh, yes, they are!" routine with the audience

Grr! Shut it! Wot d'you know anyway! (*Pompously*) I'm the king now, an' what I says goes! See! If I say it's rubbish, it's rubbish! An' they're the biggest load of old rubbish this side of [local place]!! (*To the Chorus*) Wot are ya?!
Chorus (*mumbling*) A load of rubbish.
Humpty Speak up, or I'll use my last magic wish on ya!
Chorus (*louder*) A load of rubbish, your Majesty!

Humpty hoots with mocking laughter

Humpty (*to the audience; gloatingly*) Oow! The power! (*To the Footman*) Oy! You with the candy floss on yer 'ead! I'm 'ungry again! Send fer the cook! (*He moves* L)

Footman (*calling to off* R) Summon the royal cook!
Voice (*off,* R) Summon the royal cook!

The Head Cook runs on R, *harassed, and moves straight to Humpty*

Head Cook (*grovelling*) You sent for me, your Majesty?
Humpty Yeah! I'm starvin'! I want summit to eat! And I don't want any of that muck you served up for lunch!
Head Cook That muck was my finest pâté, your Majesty.
Humpty Well, I've got news fer you! Your tatty pâté tastes like potty putty! (*He laughs at his own joke*)

The Head Cook feels obliged to join in

(*Snapping*) 'Oo said you could laugh! Watch it, Nigella! And I don't want any more of that soup! It was disgustin'! What was it?
Head Cook Cock-a-leekie
Humpty That accounts for it! You're total rubbish as a cook! There! Wot d'you say to that?
Head Cook Rissoles!
Humpty WOT?!!
Head Cook I could make you some nice rissoles, your Majesty.
Humpty Nah! Wot else you got?

The Head Cook claps his hands

Music plays

Several Junior Cooks enter R *in single file. Each one carries a tray laden with mouth-watering food — roast meats, pies, huge iced-cakes, giant jellies, etc. The Junior Cooks form a line* C

Humpty walks along the line, inspecting the food

(*To the Head Cook*) Is that all?! You'd better 'ave somethin' else, or I'll use my last wish on ya!

The Head Cook claps his hands

A very small Junior Cook enters R *carrying a tray piled high with chips*

Ah! Chips! That's more like it! (*He takes the tray and starts eating; then to the Head Cook*) Oy! Ain't you forgettin' somethin'?!

Act II, Scene 2

The Head Cook hurries across. He removes the small Juniors Cook's hat to reveal a salt shaker on his or her head. He hands it to Humpty, who sprinkles some on the chips

I won't ask where 'e keeps the ketchup!

The Head Cook replaces the shaker and the hat

(*To the other Cooks*) Well, don't just stand there! Start gettin' my dinner ready!

The Head Cook claps his hands. Music plays

All the Cooks turn and file out R. *The Head Cook and Junior Cook follow them out*

Eating, Humpty makes his way towards the thrones. He notices the litter

(*Mock horror*) What a mess! Who done that? (*To the Footman*) Get it cleaned up! Send for the royal cleaners!
Footman (*calling to off* L) Summon the royal cleaners!
Voice (*off* L) Summon the royal cleaners!

The King, Queen and Penelope enter L. *They now wear drab, tatty servants' uniforms. The King carries a broom and a small dustbin. The Queen carries a dustpan and brush*

Shaking their heads sadly, the Footman and the Chorus exit in various directions

Fiona remains, observing Humpty

King (*seeing the audience and waving to them*) Oh, hallo there! Nice to see you all again. I hope you're having a better time than we are. With all this cleaning I've got housemaid's knee, and I must say it looks better on the housemaid. Especially that little one who ——
Humpty Oy! Oy! Thas enough of that! You're not the King any more! I am! You're just a servant now! All three of ya! You only speak when you're spoken to! Got that?!
Queen This is insufferable!
Humpty (*rounding on her*) Didn't you 'ear what I said, cloth ears?!
Queen Yes.
Humpty Yes, what? Use my proper title, or I'll use my last wish on ya!
Queen Yes ... (*the ultimate pain*) your Majesty.

Humpty gloats at her humiliation

Penelope Apart from subjecting us to this humiliation, what do you want — (*contemptuously*) your Majesty?
Humpty (*indicating the mess around the throne*) This place is filthy! Get it cleaned up!

The Queen is about to protest

King (*aside to the Queen; encouraging her to comply*) Come along, my dear. Best not make him angry. Like [newsworthy person], we've just got to grin and bear it.

The King takes the Queen US. They begin to collect up the litter and put it in the dustbin. Penelope goes to assist them

Humpty (*stopping Penelope*) Not you, darlin'. I got another little job for you. These chips are a bit 'ot. I want you to blow on 'em for me. (*He takes a chip and holds it out to her*) An' no spittin'!

Indignantly, Penelope turns away

Jus' remember, sweet'eart, I can still use my last wish to make you my wife, if I want to! (*He gives an unpleasant chuckle*)

Penelope turns, glares at him, then blows on the chip. Humpty laughs and eats the chip. He holds out another, and Penelope blows on it. Humpty can offer out a chip for someone in the audience to blow on. Having collected up the litter, the King and Queen move DS

(*To the King and Queen*) Finished cleanin' up that mess?
King Yes ... er ... your Majesty.
Humpty No, you 'aven't! You've missed a bit!
King ⎫
Queen ⎭ (*looking about; together*) Where?
Humpty There! (*He throws a chip on the floor; to the Queen*) Get it cleaned up!

The Queen gets down on her knees and sweeps the chip into the dustpan. Humpty laughs and throws another chip to the floor. The Queen sweeps it up. This business is repeated a few more times, with Humpty throwing the chips at a greater distance each time, making the Queen scuttle all over the stage on her hands and knees

Act II, Scene 2

Penelope Stop this at once! In all their years as King and Queen, my parents never treated their servants in this degrading manner. It's barbaric!
Humpty Well, it's up to you, darlin'. Jus' say the word an' it can all stop. Be my wife, an' you can all go back to livin' in luxury again.
Penelope Never!
Humpty Suit yerself! (*To the King and Queen*) Oy! You two! Get upstairs and clean my bathrooms! (*With evil relish*) All eight of 'em!
Queen (*in utter misery*) Oooow!
Humpty And I wanna see my face in every single toilet bowl!
King (*to the audience*) I'd like to see that as well! (*To the Queen*) Come on, old girl! Let's go — clean round the bend!
Queen Oh, how can you make jokes!
King Not very successfully, judging by the response. Look at it this way, my love. At least we still get to be in charge of one kind of throne!

The King leads the Queen out, R

Humpty laughs and goes to eat a chip. In disgust he spits it out

Humpty Ugh! These chips are stone cold! (*He thrusts the tray at Penelope*) Get the cook to warm 'em up!

Penelope glares at him, then takes the tray and exits R

Humpty laughs, then becomes aware of Fiona watching him

Wot are you starin' at?!
Fiona I was just wondering how one person could be so unpleasant.
Humpty Practice, darlin'!
Fiona Doesn't it bother you at all? Being despised by everyone you meet?
Humpty Nope!
Fiona (*moving a little closer to him*) I don't believe that.
Humpty (*turning on her; aggressively*) Believe wot you like! Now, push off before I use my last wish on ya!
Fiona (*standing her ground*) However, I do believe that you can't be the monster you make yourself out to be. (*Slight pause*) I think you're afraid.
Humpty Wot?!
Fiona Afraid to show a different side of your personality. A side that's capable of being a decent and likeable human being.
Humpty (*wavering slightly*) What d'you ... (*Aggressively*) That's rubbish!
Fiona I don't think so. (*Moving a little closer*) What if there was someone who did like you? What would you say to them?
Humpty Huh! I'd say they needed to get their 'ead examined!
Fiona (*smiling*) Yes, perhaps I do.

Humpty Then I'd tell 'em to ... (*Reacting*) Eh?! You ... You mean ... You like me?
Fiona Yes. Despite all your faults, Humpty Dumpty, I do like you. I can't explain why, but I do. And I think you're worth saving.
Humpty Savin'? Savin' from what?
Fiona Yourself. (*Moving even closer to him*) I can help you to change, Humpty — if you'll let me try — I can help you to become a better person.
Humpty (*mulling this over*) A better person? (*To Fiona*) How?

Song 11

A song for Fiona illustrating how love will show the way. To begin with Humpty is his usual arrogant self, but during the song he gradually responds to what Fiona is trying to tell him

After the song, Fiona kisses Humpty tenderly on the cheek

Unseen by them, Jinxit enters L, *just in time to see them kiss*

Fiona parts from Humpty and moves R. *She turns to blow him a kiss, then exits*

Confused and bewitched, Humpty touches his cheek and gazes after her. Jinxit storms across to him, annoyed to say the least

Jinxit Humpty Dumpty! What is the meaning of this?!
Stop making eyes at that flighty young miss!
You took on this job to assist in my work,
Not moon around like a love-sick young jerk!
Humpty (*still in a dream*) She ... She said she likes me — No-one's ever said that to me before ... (*Touching his cheek*) She ... She kissed me too.
Jinxit It's because you're a king, a top liner!
She's nothing but a social climber!
Don't be fooled by her cunning wiles,
It's all sweet talk and the falsest of smiles.
Humpty She ... She thinks I could be a better person.
Jinxit Better than what, you dozy thing?!
You now have the power of a king!
This wretched land you hold in a fetter.
How could your life be any better?
Humpty I ... I must admit I enjoy the power ...
(*His old self showing through*)
It's nice to see 'em cringe and cower!
(*Wistfully*)
But since meeting her, per'aps it's probable,
I could be somethin' other than 'orrible.

Act II, Scene 2

Jinxit Snap out of this, you moonstruck brat!
You still work for me, don't forget that!
Forget these thoughts of changing, laddie,
And get on with your job of being a baddie!
Be warned, Humpty Dumpty! Have a care!
If you try to cross me you'd better beware!

Jinxit sweeps out L, snarling at Humpty and the audience

Humpty *(to the audience)* Crikey! I don't want to go upsettin' 'er! I'll 'ave to forget all about Fiona an' changin' my ways. *(Reverting to his old self)* I'll stay just as I am! Yeah! King Humpty Dumpty! The one they all love to hate! It's better that way! Yeah! More fun! So —— *(He snarls and jeers at the audience)* So long, you bunch of losers! Grr!

Humpty exits R

The loud honking of a horn is heard

Spit enters from L, leading Horace. Horace pulls a small decorated cart seating Patsy. She is dressed in ludicrous regal costume and wears an even bigger crown. She is honking a horn with one hand and giving the royal wave with the other. Polish brings up the rear, pushing the cart and wearing a comic number plate, i.e. Wide Load. They parade around the stage. The Chorus of Courtiers and Cooks enter and fill the back. Suddenly, Horace comes to a halt and refuses to budge

Patsy What's up? Why 'ave we stopped? What's the matter with that silly animal?
Spit I don't know, your Majesty. *(Trying to pull Horace)* Come on, Horace! Move!
Horace *(staying put and shaking his head)* Neigh! Neigh!
Polish It's probably big end trouble.
Patsy What's wrong with it's big end?
Polish Nothin'! It's yours! He's been pullin' it around the town all mornin'!
Patsy What are you inferrin', you inferior flunky?!
Polish Well, he's only a little horse, and you've got such a great big …
Patsy *(threateningly)* What?!
Polish Opinion of yerself!
Patsy *(grandly)* I wish to alight.
Spit That's what Horace wishes you were! Light!

Horace whinnies and nods his head

Patsy Get me out of this thing!

Spit and Polish engage in comic business as they haul Patsy out of the cart. Her costume is in great disarray and her crown is dislodged, etc. The duo make matters worse by trying to help her sort herself out

(*Engaging in comic business*) Oh! Look at the state I'm in! Just look at me! Just look at me!
Spit Do we really have too!
Polish You've got furniture trouble.
Patsy Furniture trouble?
Polish Yeah! Your chest has fallen into your drawers!
Spit (*engaging in comic business with Patsy's costume*) And look at this! There's a crease in yer fleece!
Polish And a kink in yer mink!
Spit There's vermin in yer ermine!
Polish And mites in yer tights!
Patsy (*pushing them away*) Get away from me! You're not 'elpin'!

Horace gives a whinnying laugh

And I shan't be usin' that fleabag nag in future! It's not dignified enough. It keeps stoppin' every five minutes to eat grass, and ... and do other things a lady doesn't mention. From now on I'll be hirin' one of those big flash libertines from [local car hire/garage]!
Spit You'd be better off hirin' a fork lift truck!

Horace and Spit and Polish laugh

Patsy Watch it! Watch it! Or I'll get my Humpty to 'ave you two decaffeinated, and yer four-legged friend turned into a pot of glue!

Horace reacts, then gallops off R with the cart. (Spit and Polish may need to assist in this)

(*To the audience; grandly giving them the royal wave*) Greetings! Greetings, my loyal objects! (*As herself*) Oh, I ain't 'alf enjoyin' bein' a queen mum! I've taken to it like a duck takes to water!

Throughout the following, Patsy chooses to ignore Spit's and Polish's interjections

Polish (*pointing to her posterior*) You can see the resemblance! (*He does a duck walk*)

Act II, Scene 2   53

Patsy Everywhere I go, the people wave and cheer.
Spit Especially when she's goin' away!
Patsy Someone said they can't wait to see my head on a stamp!
Polish No, what they said was — they can't wait to stamp on your head!
Patsy And the gorgeous gowns I get to wear! (*Showing off her costume*) What d'you think of this little number? Great, isn't it. People say it makes me look like Catherine Zeta Jones!
Spit I think they mean Tom Jones!
Patsy Oh! What it is to be so full of right royal razzamatazz!

Song 12

A comedy song and dance for Patsy, Spit and Polish and the Chorus. It ends with Patsy striking a comical pose and Spit and Polish making fun of her

Patsy chases Spit and Polish out. The Chorus etc, exit in various directions

Penelope enters from R, looking very downcast

Penelope (*to the audience; sighing*) Oh, what a sorry state of affairs. Reduced to being a servant in the very palace that was once my home. And my poor mother and father! Having to clean eight bathrooms without a single Toilet Duck to help them! I could relieve their suffering at once if I agreed to marry Humpty Dumpty. I know it's selfish of me, but the thought of becoming that little monster's wife fills me with loathing. Well, would you want to marry him? No, I thought not. And what of my darling Vince? The man I truly love! Will I ever see him again?

The Captain emerges from behind the side pillar L

Captain Just turn around and you will!
Penelope (*turning*) Vince!

Captain and Penelope rush into each other's arms

Darling, you must be careful. You've been banished from the kingdom. To return means certain death.
Captain Ah, I've consulted [local solicitors] about that. It was your father who banished me. As he is no longer the king, my banishment no longer applies.
Penelope That may be true, but it's Humpty Dumpty you now have to worry about. If he discovers you are here there is no telling what dreadful things he might do. He is threatening to use his last wish to make me his wife.

Captain Then there is only one course of action to take. You must leave here with me at once.
Penelope As much as I would love to, I can't. He keeps my parents as slaves and makes their lives a misery. I can't leave them at the mercy of that horrible little tyrant.
Captain No problem! We shall take them with us! Where are they now?
Penelope In one of the bathrooms.
Captain Then I'll take them out in a couple of shakes! Lead me to them!

Penelope takes his hand, and they run out R. *Spit and Polish enter* L, *just in time to see the lovers' departure*

Spit (*looking off* R) Hey! That was the captain!
Polish Cor! 'E won't 'alf cop it. 'E shouldn't be back 'ere! 'E's been varnished!
Spit Banished, you clot!
Polish That as well! What d'you reckon 'e's up to?
Spit How should I know!
Polish (*indicating the audience*) Let's ask our mates out there. They must know what's goin' on. If they've been awake!
Spit (*to the audience*) Hi, folks! Do you know why the captain's come back? What's he up to? (*By-play with the audience*) He's goin' to take Penelope and her mum and dad away? Good for him!

Humpty enters R, *in time to hear the next line. He creeps up behind them*

Polish Yeah! That's great news! Let's 'ope 'orrible 'Umpty doesn't find out!
Spit Oh, he won't. He's not here. (*To the audience*) Is he, folks?

"Yes!" from the audience

Spit
Polish } (*together; reacting with fear*) W — where?

The duo engage with the "He's behind you!" routine. They turn around and Humpty keeps behind them, etc. Eventually they come face to face. Spit and Polish yell, and recoil L

Humpty What shouldn't I find out about?!
Spit Er — that [topical media personality] is coming to live in [local place]!
Polish Yeah! He/she wanted to live in [another local place], but they've already got their quota of oddballs! [Or topical gag to suit]
Humpty Don't give me that load of rubbish! (*Advancing on them; threateningly*) You two know somethin'! What is it? Tell me!

Act II, Scene 2

Spit There's nothing to tell! We don't know anything! Anything at all! (*To Polish*) Do we?!
Polish No! We're two picnics short of a sandwich!
Humpty (*to the audience*) I bet you rotten lot are in on this! You tell me! Come on!
Spit They don't know anything either. They're as ignorant as we are!
Polish Yeah! (*Pointing someone out*) 'Specially that one, pickin' his nose!
Humpty (*to them; menacingly*) I'm warnin' you! If you don't tell me what's goin' on, I'm gonna use my last magic wish on you!
Spit \
Polish } (*together; cringing*) Oh, no!!
Humpty Oh, yes, I am! I wish ...
Spit \
Polish } (*together; wailing*) We'll tell! We'll tell!
Humpty (*with an evil chuckle*) I thought you might! Well?!
Spit Captain Valiant has come back!
Humpty And?!
Polish That's all we know!
Humpty I reckon not! (*Menacingly*) I wish ...
Spit All right! He's going to take Penelope and her parents away with him!
Humpty (*enraged*) Oh, 'e is, is 'e! We'll see about that! Where is 'e now?! Which way did 'e go?!

Spit and Polish exchange quick glances

Spit \
Polish } (*together; pointing off* L) That way!
Humpty Tryin' to steal my fiancée, is 'e! I'll soon sort 'im out!!

Snarling, Humpty storms out L

Spit Quick! Let's go and warn the captain!

Spit and Polish rush towards the R *exit*

Patsy enters R

Spit and Polish pull up short

Patsy Ah!
Spit \
Polish } (*together; recoiling*) Ahhgh!!
Patsy 'Ave you seen my stripling?

Polish No, thanks! Not on an empty stomach!
Patsy I'm talkin' about my son! Your salubrious sovereign! King Humpty Dumpty!
Spit
Polish } (*pointing* L) He went that way!
Patsy I'll just rest my royal rump on the rostrum ready for 'is regal return! (*She goes* US *and sits on one of the thrones*)

Polish looks off R, *and gets in a panic*

Polish (*to Spit; in frantic undertones*) Oh, no! Here comes the captain with the others! What are we gonna do?! Don't panic! Don't panic!
Spit Run and stop them! I'll try and divert her attention.

Spit pushes Polish

Polish runs out R

(*To Patsy; as he moves up*) I hope you're pleased with the royal garden make-over? (*He looks out of the window* R) I must say they're doing a marvellous job. Wouldn't you like to see how well it's coming on?
Patsy (*huffily*) No, thanks. I'm not interested any more! I wanted the "Ground Force" team to do it! But it seems Charlie Dimmock's got wedged in a water feature, and Tommy Walsh is 'avin' problems with 'is pergola!

Polish creeps back on from R, *unseen by Patsy. He signals to Spit*

Spit (*getting a brainwave and looking out of the window again*) Oh, look! I'm sure I just saw Alan Titchmarsh out there!
Patsy (*now very interested and jumping up*) Alan Titchmarsh! (*To the audience*) Oh, girls! That man can prick out my seedlings any time 'e likes! (*Excitedly rushing to join Spit at the window*) Oh, where is 'e?! Where is 'e?!! (*She looks out of the window with her back to the audience*) Where's Alan?!
Spit He's just gone behind that bush.

Patsy continues to look. Spit signals to Polish, who signals to off R

The Captain creeps on, followed by Penelope and the King and Queen. They start to tiptoe across the stage towards the exit L

When they are about half-way across, Patsy speaks and they all freeze

Act II, Scene 2   57

Patsy (*still looking out of the window*) Why's 'e takin' so long? What is he doin' behind that bush? (*She is about to turn around*)
Spit (*quickly preventing her from turning*) Keep looking! He'll come out in a minute!

Patsy looks out of the window, Spit signals to the others and they continue to creep towards the L exit. They nearly make their escape

> *Humpty enters L. He is followed by two of the King's Men and several of the Chorus*

Humpty Not so fast, soldier boy!
Patsy (*coming down*) Humpty, my sweet! What's all this hassle in our castle?
Humpty (*mockingly*) The great Captain Fantastic's come back! And 'e's tryin' to steal my fiancée!
Captain I'm not trying to, Humpty Dumpty, I'm going to! (*To Penelope, the King and Queen*) RUN FOR IT!!

The Captain and the others run towards the exit R. They stop in their tracks

> *Two more of the King's Men and the rest of the Chorus enter R. Fiona is with them*

Humpty struts over to the Captain, roaring with mocking laughter

Humpty Ha! Ha! Ha! You're trapped, soldier boy! You're completely in my power!
Captain Not yet!

The Captain leaps at Humpty and grabs him by his collar and the seat of his pants. General reaction. Patsy screams

> Do you know what I'm going to do, you obnoxious little tyrant? I'm going to throw you out of the window! Right into the palace moat!

The Captain drags the struggling Humpty to the edge of the stage and prepares to throw him over

> (*To the audience*) Shall I? Shall I do it?

"Yes! Do it! Go on!" etc, etc! from the audience

Patsy Ooooh!! Stop 'im! 'E's gonna drop my Humpty in it!

Fiona (*rushing to the Captain and pleading desperately*) No, Captain! ... Don't! ... Please! ... Don't!!
Humpty (*dangling over the edge*) You'd better listen to her, soldier boy! You can throw me out of this window if you like, but on the way down I can still use my last wish to destroy this kingdom and everyone in it!

There is general shock horror from the others

Penelope He means it, Vince!

The Captain hesitates, then pulls Humpty back from the edge and releases him. Patsy rushes to fuss over him

Humpty (*pushing her away; pointing to the Captain and the others*) Seize them!

The King's Men take charge of the Captain and the others

Penelope What are you going to do to us?
Humpty I 'aven't made up me mind yet, darlin'. Meanwhile I'll put you somewhere where you can't run away. (*To the King's Men*) Take 'em to the palace dungeons and lock 'em up!
Queen (*in total misery*) Oh, no! First the bathrooms — now the dungeons!
King Out of the lavatory pan into the mire!
Humpty (*to the Men*) Take them away!

The Captain, the King and Queen and Penelope are taken out L by the King's Men

Fiona approaches Humpty

Fiona (*on the verge of tears*) I — I thought you were going to change, I really did!

Bursting into tears, Fiona runs out R

Affected and confused by Fiona, Humpty turns to watch her tearful departure

Patsy (*rushing across to fuss over Humpty*) Oh, Humpty! Humpty! Are you all right after all that tough and rubble? Did that nasty man hurt my little treasure?! Let Mummy kiss it better.
Humpty (*pulling away*) Leave me alone!

Act II, Scene 3   59

Patsy Oh, 'e's upset. (*She leads him up to the thrones*) You come and 'ave a nice sit down with Mummy. (*She sits on one of the thrones and takes Humpty on to her lap*) There! Now you 'ave a little resty-poohs. (*To the Chorus*) Well, don't just stand there like rejects from [TV game show]! Your king needs cheerin' up! Get on with it!

Song 13 (Reprise of Song 10)

During the Chorus reprise, Patsy tries to comfort Humpty, but his mind is obviously troubled by Fiona's parting words. The number ends, and the Lights fade to black-out

Scene change music

SCENE 3

A Dungeon Cell

Very dark and gloomy lighting comes up. A front-cloth shows grim stone walls with a high barred window, manacles and chains, etc. There is one rough bench UR

An eerie spotlight comes up DL

Jinxit enters into the spotlight. She is full of glee and is cackling evilly

Jinxit   Hee! Hee! Things are really getting warm,
                  Now that Humpty's returned to norm.
                  I made him see he was in error,
                  Now he's back to his reign of terror!
                  The captain's plan he foiled so well.
                  They'll soon be locked up in this cell!
                  And he still has one wish up his sleeve!
                  On that happy note — I will take my leave!

Cackling, Jinxit exits DL

The lighting becomes brighter. The sound of a heavy door creaking open is heard off DR

The Queen, distraught, enters DR. *She is supported by the King. The Captain and Penelope follow*

The sound of the door clanging shut is heard off DR. *The Queen lets out a pitiful wail*

King (*spotting the audience and waving to them*) Hallo, there! Oh, dear! I see you've been dumped in the dungeon as well, eh? It's going to be a bit of a squeeze! Jolly good job we're all friends, what! (*He laughs*)

The Queen lets out another pitiful wail

Now, now. Don't upset yourself, old girl! Keep yer chin up! All three of 'em.

Queen (*rounding on him*) Don't tell *me* what to do! And don't call me *old* girl! This is all your fault! I told you not to aggravate that Humpty Dumpty! But would you listen to me? Oh, no! And this is the result! Reduced to being commoners and locked up in one of our own dungeon cells! And not even a south-facing one! I dread to think what he plans to do to us now! (*Rounding on the Captain*) And as for *you*! Call yourself a soldier! Huh!

Penelope Don't take it out on Vince. Even though he was banished, he gallantly came back to rescue us under pain of death.

King That's true! (*Shaking hands with the Captain*) Thank you for that, Captain.

Queen (*exploding*) What are you thanking him for?! He didn't rescue us, did he! He just made matters worse!

King Well, it's the thought that counts.

Queen And what would you know about that?! You haven't had a thought for years!

King ⎫ ⎧ Now look here! There's no need for that! I won't have
      (*together*) that! (*etc.*)
Queen ⎭ ⎩ You're hopeless! Hopeless! You've always been hopeless! (*etc.*)

Captain (*loudly*) Please!

The King and Queen go silent

Thank you. I think we should stop bickering among ourselves and try to think of a way out of this.

King Spoken like a true soldier. What do you suggest?

Captain (*shrugging*) I — I don't know.

Queen Huh! Spoken like a useless great twit!

King My dear, that's rather coarse language for you, isn't it?

Queen (*cynically adopting a heavy Cockney* [or local accent]) Gor blimey! Wot ya expect! Fanks to you, I'm as common as muck na! Ain't I, me ole cock sparras? Sorted! (*She starts laughing hysterically, then dissolves into tears*)

Act II, Scene 3

Gently, the King takes her to the bench, and sits her down. He then returns to the others

King (*in hushed tones*) We've got to do something fast. The poor old girl's getting historical.
Captain (*looking about*) If only there were some way of breaking out of this dungeon.
King (*shaking his head*) Impossible! It's like me. Too well built. We'll just have to sit it out, I suppose. This dungeon isn't so bad once you get used to it. Quite cosy, in fact. I've been in far worse places. The [local reference] for instance.

The Captain takes Penelope's hand

Captain At least there's one thing that we can be grateful for.
Penelope (*as if she didn't know*) What's that, Vince?
Captain We're still together.

Song 14 (Optional)

Note: If more time is required for the scene change, a song can be introduced here with follow-spots etc.

Captain Shh! Listen! What's that?

They listen. The door is heard creaking open

King Sounds like someone in need of WD 40.
Penelope (*pointing* DR) Look! The door's opening!
Captain Perhaps it's a rescue party!

Spit and Polish enter DR

King Wrong! It's the Monster Raving Loony Party! [Or some other political reference]
Captain Spit and Polish!
Spit
Polish } (*together; snapping to attention and saluting*) Sah!
Captain At ease! What are you doing here? Have you come to let us out?

There is the sound of the door clanging shut

Spit 'Fraid not, Captain. We've been sent to join you.

Polish Yeah! We've been nobbled, nabbed an' nicked!
Captain Is this because you tried to help us escape?
Spit ⎫
Polish ⎭ (*together*) Y'sah!
Captain I haven't forgotten that. Well done, men!
Spit ⎫
Polish ⎭ (*together; very pleased with themselves*) Thank you, sah!
Captain (*sternly*) Just as I haven't forgotten that this is all your fault in the first place! If you two hadn't broken that wretched egg and released Humpty Dumpty, none of us would be in this confounded mess!
Spit But it's as I told you before, sah. It wasn't our fault.
Polish No! It was that weird lookin' woman, sah! She tricked us!
Queen What weird looking woman?
Polish We don't know 'er name, but she's really 'orrible!
Spit And we reckon she's in league with Humpty Dumpty!
Captain Well, it now appears we have another problem to face. That tyrant Humpty Dumpty has got an accomplice!
Penelope But who is she?

There is a flash. The lighting becomes brighter. There are startled reactions from the others

Captain (*pointing* DR) Look! The door's open!

They all gape in amazement

Queen (*rounding on the King*) Well, don't just stand there! Let's get out of here!

The Queen rushes out DR, *followed by the others. The Good Fairy enters from* DL

Good Fairy (*to the audience*)
          For better or worse I have set them free,
          But how they will fare I cannot foresee.

Cackling, Jinxit sweeps on DL

Jinxit   Then let me tell you, my incompetent mate!
                   You've doomed them all to a hideous fate!
                   Young Humpty is going to have a ball!
                   With his last wish, he'll destroy them all!
Good Fairy Don't be so sure. Don't rush your fences.
                   I still think Humpty will come to his senses.

Act II, Scene 4

Jinxit I still believe he will see the light,
And do in the end what he knows to be right.
Oh, change the record! Stop that yearning!
I tell you, Humpty Dumpty is not for turning!
I wonder what his plans will be,
For those six fools that you set free?
I hope it's something really gory!
And a gruesome ending to this story!
I dare not miss a single fraction!
I must away — to watch the action!
Hee! Hee! Hee!!

Cackling evilly, Jinxit sweeps out DL

The Good Fairy addresses the audience

Good Fairy Do not worry, my patient friends,
You too shall see how the story ends.
Be you local folk or from over the borders,
All will be revealed before they call "last orders".

The Good Fairy waves her wand, and the Lights fade to black-out

Scene change music

SCENE 4

Eggton-On-Sea

Song 15

The Chorus and Children, as holiday-makers, are discovered in song and dance. Horace is with them

After the number, Patsy, wearing yet another ridiculous regal outfit, enters UL. *She pushes her way through the Chorus to* C

Patsy Move! Out the way! Mind yer backs! Move! (*Grandly*) Your wonderful King will be 'ere at any moment! So — on your knees!

Grumbling, all the Chorus kneel. Horace remains standing

(*To Horace*) That goes for you an' all, Shergar! On yer knees!

With comic business, Horace kneels with his front legs, while his hind legs remain standing

(*Going to Horace*) All four of 'em! All four of em'! (*She slaps Horace's rear*) Come on! Get the boot down!

With comic business, Horace lowers and settles his rear end

(*To the Chorus, grandly gesturing to* L) And now! Here he is! That precious pint-sized potentate! That marvellous mini Monarch of the Glen! Your own — your very own — King Humpty Dumpty! Hip Hip Hurray! (*She starts clapping and cheering*)

Humpty enters from L *and moves* C. *He has none of his old arrogant swagger, and appears thoughtful and distracted*

Patsy (*indicating the Chorus*) They're all ready for you, sweetie. All ready to be treated like the revolting riff-raff they are!
Humpty (*just glancing at the Chorus*) Send 'em away.
Patsy (*dismayed*) What?! Y'mean, you don't want to treat 'em like scum? You don't want to treat 'em like [local rival football team] supporters?
Humpty No.
Patsy I see. (*Slight pause*) Can I do it then?
Humpty (*firmly*) No, just send them away (*He moves away to* DL)
Patsy (*puzzled*) Oh! (*To the audience*) 'E must be sickenin' fer somethin'! (*To the Chorus*) Well, you 'eard 'is royal nibs! Go away! Clear off!

The Chorus rise and beat hasty exits in all directions

Horace remains kneeling

(*Moving to Horace*) You too! Come on, you lazy four-legged layabout! Up ya get!

With comic business, Patsy gets Horace to his feet. She has to put her shoulder under his hind quarters and push him up

(*To the audience*) Cor! It's the first time I've backed a horse this way! (*To Horace*) Gee up! Get out of 'ere! Shoo!

Horace trots US

(*Moving to Humpty; with concern*) What's the matter with Mummy's little soldier? You seem down in the dumps. Shall Mummy get you summit to eat? It must be all of five minutes since you last filled oows ickle tumsy wumsy.

Humpty I'm not 'ungry.
Patsy *(with amazement)* Not 'ungry! *(To the audience)* 'E is sickenin' fer somethin'! *(To Humpty)* What is it then, my sugar plum? Tell your old mummy all about it. *(She goes to cuddle him)*
Humpty *(brushing her aside and moving* C*)* Leave me alone. I wanna think.
Patsy *(following him)* Think? Oh, you don't need to do that any more, my dove. You're royalty now. You need never think another thunk again.
Humpty What 'appened to my broken eggshell? Is it still in there? *(He indicates the B&B)*
Patsy I suppose so. Why d'you want to know that?
Humpty I've got an idea.

Humpty exits into the B&B

Patsy *(to the audience; puzzled)* Getting' ideas! Thinkin'! 'E's defiantly not actin' like a royal! *(She rushes towards the B&B)* Humpty! Wait for Mummy! Humpty!

Patsy exits into the B&B. Horace watches her go, then trots out R

Jinxit enters L, *snarling at the audience. She looks off* R, *then quickly hides* UL. *The King and Queen peep around the wall* R. *They look cautiously about, then creep on*

King It's all right, old thing. There's nobody about — except our friends out there. *(To the audience)* There's no-one here, is there?

Jinxit emerges from hiding and creeps up behind them

The audience start shouting warnings of "Behind you!", etc. The King and Queen turn around and Jinxit keeps behind them. This routine continues until eventually, Jinxit creeps out DL

(To the audience) Right! We'll be ready for 'em this time!

Spit and Polish creep on backwards from UL

(To the Queen; in hushed tones) Turn on the count of three. One — two — three!

They both turn quickly and grab the unsuspecting Spit and Polish. The Queen gives them a good battering, until the King stops her

Steady on, Rocky! It's only Ant and Dec! [Or other duo]
Queen *(to them)* How dare you sneak up and try to take us unaware!

Polish I never touched yer underwear!
Spit Where's the captain?
Queen Where's Penelope?
Polish We thought they were with you!
King We thought they were with you!
Spit We haven't seen them since we out of the dungeon.
Polish (*to the audience*) Have you seen the captain and Penelope, folks?

"No!" from the audience

Queen (*panicking*) Oh, my little girl! My only daughter! What has become of her! Ooow!!
King Steady on, old girl. Don't get yer knickers in a knot! She's all right. She's with the captain.
Queen That's what worries me! And kindly do not mention my knick... My unmentionables in public!

Horace enters from L

Polish Look! There's Horace! Perhaps he's seen them!

Polish and Spit collect Horace, and bring him DS

Spit Have you seen the captain and Princess Penelope, Horace?
Horace (*shaking his head*) Neigh!
Polish Are you sure?

Horace nods

Queen Oh, this is ridiculous! How can you expect that stupid dumb animal to know anything!

Horace reacts to this with disdain

King Don't say that, old thing! He's a very intelligent gee gee.
Queen Mm. Compared to you, I suppose he is!
King Yes. (*With a double take*) What? (*To Horace*) Now then, old chap. Can you tell us what's happening?

Horace nods, then trots over to the B&B. He indicates for them to look inside. They all approach the B&B, look through the window, then converse in hushed tones

Polish It's Humpty Dumpty!
Spit And his mum!

Act II, Scene 4

Queen What are they doing?
King They're coming out!
Polish Quick! We'd better hide!

They all scuttle away and hide behind the wall L. Flustered, Horace trots around in a circle

Patsy and Humpty come out of the B&B. They carry the pieces of broken eggshell

Trapped, Horace tries to adopt a nonchalant air with crossed hooves

Patsy Oh! That four-legged fleabag is still 'ere! (*To Horace*) 'Aven't you got any stables to go to?

Horace nods his head

Then do it!

Humpty and Patsy turn away to put the pieces of shell on the ground below the B&B. While they are doing this, Spit and Polish emerge from hiding and beckon to Horace

Spit
Polish } (*together*) Horace! Horace

Horace sees them. Spit and Polish vanish from sight just as Humpty and Patsy turn around

Patsy What was that? I thought I 'eard voices!
Humpty So did I. It seemed to be comin' from over there. (*To the audience*) Is there someone 'idin'?

Horace shakes his head at the audience, indicating for them to say "No"

"No!" from the audience

Patsy (*to the audience*) Oh, yes there is!

"Oh! no there isn't!" routine with the audience

Well, I don't believe you! I'm gonna take a look! (*She marches* L)

With comic business, Horace keeps trotting up and down, getting in her way and preventing her from going to L

Oooh! Get out of the way!

Horace gives her a hefty push and she falls over. With comic business, Humpty helps her to stand. During this, Spit and Polish emerge from hiding and beckon to Horace

Spit
Polish } (*together*) Horace! Horace!

Humpty and Patsy hear. Spit and Polish vanish from sight as they turn around

Humpty There it is again! I'm gonna look this time! You hold on to that horse!

Gingerly, Patsy takes hold of Horace's bridle. He has his head facing her. Humpty creeps towards the wall L. *Just as he gets there, Horace sneezes loudly, right in Patsy's face. Patsy reacts. Humpty stops and looks back. Horace sneezes again*

Patsy Ugh! 'E sneezed all over me! Ugh! Ugh!!
Humpty That must be what we heard! There's no-one there! It was just the horse sneezin'.
Patsy (*to Horace*) Was it you?

Horace nods, then sneezes over her again

Ooooh! Right in me eye! Ugh!!
Humpty Take it away!
Patsy Me? Where?
Humpty Anywhere!
Patsy (*to Horace*) Right, you! Come on!

Patsy leads Horace towards the exit DR. *Horace sneezes again, this time in the direction of the audience*

(*To the audience*) That'll teach you to want front row seats! (*To Horace*) Did no-one ever tell you to put yer hoof in front yer mouth?

Patsy leads Horace out, accompanied by another sneeze

Act II, Scene 4

Humpty crosses and watches them go. He then looks down at the pieces of eggshell, deep in thought. While his back is turned, Spit, Polish and the King and Queen emerge from hiding. They cautiously creep out DL

A slight pause

Fiona enters L

Fiona sees Humpty, and is about to exit the way she came, when he turns and sees her

Humpty Fiona — wait ...

Fiona stops, but keeps her back turned to him

(*Moving over*) Can I speak to you — please.
Fiona And say what? (*She turns to face him*) More lies? Like how you wanted to become a better person when you had no intention of doing so.
Humpty Let me explain ...
Fiona Don't bother!

Tearfully, Fiona runs out L

Jinxit sweeps on R

Jinxit Are you still wasting time with that young filly! All your prisoners are free to run willy nilly!
Humpty (*confused and distracted*) Free? W ... What d'you mean?
Jinxit That good fairy is back! She worked a spell! She's released them all from the dungeon cell!
Humpty (*still distracted*) Er ...
Jinxit Don't just stand there, dumb and gaping! After them quick, and stop 'em escaping!
Humpty Oh ... Yeah!

Humpty runs out L. *With a snarl at the audience, Jinxit follows him out*

The Captain and Penelope creep on R

Penelope What are we going to do, Vince?
Captain By now Humpty Dumpty will know of our escape. He'll be searching for us. We must find the others and get as far away from here as possible. (*Slight pause*) Darling, brace yourself. We might even have to go as far away as — [local place]!

Penelope (*reacting*) Oh, no! Not that primitive, desolate place!
Captain I'm afraid so, but I've heard it's not so bad since they had water laid on [or topical local gag].
Penelope I wonder where the others can be. Oh, Vince, you don't think they've been recaptured, do you?
Captain I hope not, but ... (*He looks off* L) Look out! Here comes Humpty Dumpty! Quick, let's hide! (*He looks about*) In there!

Captain and Penelope run into the B&B

Humpty enters from L, *with four of the King's Men. Jinxit follows at a short distance, keeping a watch on Humpty*

Humpty (*to the King's Men*) I want you to search this side of the town for the escaped prisoners. Search every street. Every building. You two take that side. (*He indicates* L)

Two of the King's Men salute and run out L

(*To the other two King's Men*) You come with me. (*He moves* DS, *dithering and unsure how to proceed*)

Jinxit comes down to join him

Jinxit Humpty, I think you're in need of a little guiding.
(*She points to the audience*)
I bet they know where the fugitives are hiding!
Humpty Oh ... Yeah! ... (*To the audience; politely for him*) Do you know where they are?

"No!" from the audience

Humpty (*to Jinxit*) They don't know.
Jinxit (*with annoyance*) Bah! That's no way to treat this trash!
You've got to threaten 'em — hard and brash!
(*Snarling at the audience*)
Come on! Tell us where they are, you nits,
Or I'll come down there and smash you to bits!
Are they in there?! (*She points to B&B*)

"No!" from the audience

You can't fool me! I know your game!
In every panto it's always the same!

Act II, Scene 4   71

> (*To Humpty*) It's very simple. Can't you guess?!
> When they say "no", they really mean "yes"!
> They're hiding — (*pointing to the B&B*) in there!

Cackling, she sweeps into the B&B. Humpty and the two King's Men follow her off

To suitable music, a chase sequence follows. Strobe lighting can be used

The King and Queen run on DL, *hotly pursued by one of the King's Men and some of the Chorus and Children. They are chased around the stage, then out* UR. *Spit and Polish run on from* DR, *hotly pursued by the other King's Men and the rest of the Chorus and Children. They are chased around the stage, then out* U L. *Still pursued, the King and Queen run on from* UR. *They are chased around the stage. Still pursued, Spit and Polish run on from* UL. *It soon becomes a confused muddle. Who is chasing who?! Fugitive or pursuer? To add to the confusion, Horace trots on and becomes part of the mêlée. At one point they all stop to get their breath back, then carry on with the chase. Patsy enters and gets drawn into the mad whirl. It ends with her spinning around like a top and falling over. The fugitives are chased out* DL *by the two King's Men. Horace does a few dizzy spins, then trots out after them*

The chase music stops and the lighting returns to normal

Patsy staggers to her feet and comes forward

Patsy Crikey! Talk about 'avin' a funny turn, girls! What was that all about? People runnin' around everywhere! 'Ave I missed summit? The [local event] 'asn't started already, 'as it? Where's my precious boy got to now? Humpty! (*Calling, she moves to the B&B*) Per'aps 'e went back in 'ere.

Patsy goes into the B&B

Humpty, are you in there, sweetie?

A slight pause

A loud commotion, yells, screams, crashes and bangs, etc. is heard coming from inside the B&B

The two King's Men enter from the B&B, dragging on a bedraggled Patsy. She is kicking and screaming

Patsy (*yelling*) Ooow!! Let me go!! How dare you!! Ooow!!

Humpty comes out of the B&B, followed by Jinxit

(*To him*) Oooh! Humpty! Make 'em take their mucky maulers off yer mummy!

Humpty signals to the King's Men and they release Patsy

Humpty, what's goin' on?! It's worse than a Saturday night at the [local pub/club]! (*Business with her costume*) Just look at the state of me loose covers!
1st King's Man (*to her*) We thought you were one the escaped prisoners, your Majesty.
2nd King's Man (*to her*) We've very sorry, your Majesty.
Patsy I should think so an' all. I've been mauled, mistreated an' manhandled! (*Aside to one of the King's Men*) If you want to do it again, I'm free tomorrow night. Ten o'clock behind the soap factory! [Or local works]

The King and Queen, Spit and Polish are pushed on from DL by the other King's Men

General reaction

3rd King's Man Your Majesty, we've caught four of them.
Humpty What about the others?
4th King's Man They're still at large, your Majesty.
Jinxit Humpty, where is that brain of yours residing?
Get them to tell you where the others are hiding!
Patsy She's right! (*She double takes and reacts to Jinxit*) Crikey! What's [topical nasty] doin' 'ere!
King I say! (*To Spit and Polish*) Is that the weird looking woman you were telling us about?
Spit
Polish } (*together*) That's her!
Queen Ugh! What a revolting looking person!
Jinxit Well, you're no [current female "looker"] believe you me!
Now tell us! Where's the captain and Penelope?
Others We don't know.
Jinxit They lie!
(*To Humpty*) Don't just stand there, you gormless youth!
Threaten 'em with your wish to extract the truth!
Humpty Oh, yeah! ... (*To the others*) Tell me where the others are, or I'll use my last wish on you! Where are they?

Act II, Scene 4

King We just told you. We don't know.
Queen And we wouldn't tell you even if we did!
Spit \
Polish / (*together*) So there!
Humpty (*to the others*) Right! This is yer last chance! Tell me where they are.

With comic business, the King, Queen, Spit and Polish close their eyes, stiffen their sinews, and prepare for the worst. Jinxit urges Humpty to continue

You asked for it! I wish ...

The Captain and Penelope enter from the B&B

Captain Stop! That will not be necessary. Here we are!

General reaction. The King, Queen, Spit and Polish sigh with relief and relax. The Captain and Penelope cross over and join them

Jinxit (*to Humpty, seething*) They've made you look an utter fool!
          Avenge yourself with something cruel!
          Cause Penelope some grief and strife!
          Use your wish to make her — your wife!

General reaction

Captain (*to Jinxit; nonchalantly*) I hate to disappoint you, but I'm afraid he can't do that. Because, you see — Penelope is already married. To me!

More general reaction

Penelope As soon as we got out of the dungeon we went straight to a Justice of the Peace who married us on the spot. (*She proudly links arms with the Captain*) You are now looking at Captain and Mrs Valiant.
Queen (*appalled*) Oh, no! My daughter married to military menial!
Penelope You forget, Mama, I'm just a commoner now. We all are.
King She's quite right, old girl. Nothing you can do about it. (*He turns to kiss Penelope and shake hands with the Captain*) Well done! Congratulations!

Spit and Polish join in with the congratulations

Jinxit (*to the Humpty*) Again they've made you look a clown!
          Will you take this lying down?!

> Don't let this be your decline and fall.
> Use your wish — to destroy them all!

Horrified reaction and uproar from all the others. Jinxit sweeps away R, and stands close to the pieces of broken eggshell

Fiona No! — Humpty, you mustn't ... Don't listen to her!
Jinxit (*with a loud snarl*) Silence!!

The others go silent

> Humpty Dumpty, I am still your master!
> To cross me now would court disaster.
> If you refuse to destroy this crew,
> I will do it myself, and that includes — you!!

General reaction

Humpty All right ... All right ... I'll do it!
Fiona (*pleading*) Humpty! No!
Humpty (*snarling at her; his old obnoxious self*) Shut it, you! (*To Jinxit*) You're right. They did try to make me look a fool! No-one does that to King Humpty Dumpty an' gets away wiv it! (*Addressing the others*) You're all gonna pay fer what you've done! And pay dearly — with yer lives!

Horrified responses from the others

I'm sick of this dump anyway! As soon as I've blown it off the face of the earth, I'll find somewhere else to terrorize. (*To the audience*) That rotten lot in [local place] will do fer starters!
Jinxit (*cackling with delight*) Hee! Hee! Hee!
> I knew you'd see sense and work to my rules!
> Now hurry up! Destroy these fools!

Humpty (*addressing the others; menacingly*) Right! 'Ere goes!

Terrified, they all cower and cling to each other, preparing for the ultimate horror

> At being a real nasty I hope to excel!
> I wish ... (*he suddenly turns and points to Jinxit*) You were inside that giant eggshell!

There is a flash, followed by a complete black-out. Magical music plays. Confused cries are heard coming from the others. A loud, echoing scream comes from Jinxit. This gradually diminishes into silence

Act II, Scene 4

Jinxit vanishes in the black-out

The lighting returns to normal, and the music fades out. In a spotlight, in Jinxit's place, stands the egg—fully restored! There is complete silence as everyone gazes at the egg in mute astonishment, then everyone breaks into excited chatter

King By Jove! I must say that was a pretty nifty trick, young Humpty! The old bat certainly didn't see that one comin'!
Humpty I 'ad to pretend I was still on 'er side, or she'd 'ave carried out 'er threat an' destroyed us all.
Fiona Humpty — does this mean you're ... you're ...
Humpty Yes, Fiona. I've now become the better person you thought I was.

General reaction

Fiona (*rushing to Humpty*) Oh, Humpty!

Humpty and Fiona embrace

Others (*sighing*) Ahh!
Humpty (*to all, including the audience*) Folks, I just want to say how truly sorry I am for my disgustin' behaviour in the past. I know I don't deserve your forgiveness, but ... but could you please find it in your 'earts to give me a second chance. Please.
Patsy (*tearfully*) Oooh, I'm fillin' up! It's just like [TV soap]! (*Pleading to the others and to the audience*) Oh, please say you'll give 'im a second chance! Pleeeease!!

All the others confer, then unanimously nod their consent

King (*to Humpty*) Well, you've got your second chance, young fella.
Humpty Thanks, your Majesty.
King Your Majesty? But ...
Humpty I hereby renounce the throne along with my old ways. (*He takes off his crown and hands it to the King*) 'Ere you go. Welcome back, your Majesty!

The King puts on the crown. Everyone cheers. The Queen comes forward

Queen (*to Humpty*) Ahem!!
Humpty Oh, yeah! (*He takes the crown off Patsy's head and gives it to the Queen*)

The Queen puts the crown on

Patsy (*to the audience; resigned*) Oh, well! It was nice while it lasted, folks! It's back to bein' as common as muck, I suppose.
Humpty Sorry, Mum.
Patsy (*reacting*) Mum?! Does that mean you still want me to be your mummy?
Humpty If you'll 'ave me.
Patsy Well, I ... Oh, sweetie-pie!! Come to Mummy!!

Patsy throws her arms around Humpty and they embrace

Others (*sighing*) Ahh!!
Patsy (*to Humpty; very sweetly*) Cherub, d'you mind if Mummy does somethin' she's been wantin' to do for ages?
Humpty No. What?
Patsy This!

She slaps his bottom. The others roar their approval and laugh

Humpty (*to the audience*) I guess I 'ad that comin'!
Queen (*to Humpty; sternly*) And what, may I ask, do you propose to do about that?! (*She points to the egg*)

All the others turn to look across at the egg

King By jove, yes! That rotten old egg!
Queen (*to Humpty*) It is your property, and we certainly don't want it here any longer. The wretched thing has caused enough trouble.

The others agree

King I'm afraid she's right, Humpty. We can't have it gettin' broken and that frightful witch gettin' out, can we? What are you goin' to do with it?
Humpty (*at a loss*) I —I don't know ...
Captain May I suggest we take it — very, very carefully — out of the kingdom, and just leave it somewhere?
Queen That sounds like an excellent idea!

The others think so too

Penelope But that's no good. If we did that we'll only be putting some other poor, unsuspecting kingdom at risk.

Act II, Scene 4   77

Others (*gloomily*) That's true!
Patsy Per'aps our friends out there can 'elp! (*To the audience*) 'Ave you got any suggestions where we can put it?

Comic by-play and ad-libs with the audience. This develops into a noisy, heated argument amongst the Principals and Chorus

There is a flash

> *The Good Fairy appears from* DR. *If desired some small Fairies can accompany her. She moves to the egg*

Stunned silence from the others

Good Fairy   Please do not have a revolution.
To your dilemma I have the solution.
This egg in fact belongs to me.
It is strictly fairy property.
I will take it through the magic portals,
And remove it from this land of mortals.
But before I do that, I want to bid,
A fond farewell to this special kid.
(*She crosses to Humpty*)
Humpty Dumpty, I always knew,
There was a better person inside of you.
Today you have proved to these adults and tots,
That a leopard is capable of changing its spots.
(*To the audience*) The moral of this story clearly displays,
It's never too late to change your ways.
(*To Humpty*) Goodbye, Humpty I wish you well.
Now to remove this unwanted shell.
(*She goes back to the egg, and raises her wand*)

Magical music plays under

> O! Powers of goodness, I now invoke!
> Remove this egg with its evil yolk.
> Take it hence with spell and charm,
> To a place where it can do no harm!
> (*She waves her wand over the egg*)

There is a flash, followed by a complete Black-out

The Good Fairy, small Fairies and egg vanish

The lighting returns to normal. There are general reactions of delight

Patsy (*to the audience*) Cor! What about that! Wasn't she good! Harry Potter, eat yer 'eart out!

General excited chatter from everyone

Queen Silence!

They all go silent

I have an announcement to make.
King (*to the audience*) Ugh! Here comes the wet blanket! (*To her; fearing the worst*) Yes, dear?
Queen (*sternly*) Now that everything has been settled, I think we should all ... (*Jubilantly waving her arms*) Celebrate!! (*She throws her arms around the much-surprised King*)
All (*cheering*) Hurrah!!

They all go into a lively song and dance

Song 16

After the song, a front-cloth used in ACT 1, SCENE 3, *is lowered*

SCENE 5

A Spot of Yolk Singing

Spit and Polish enter, doing their comic march. They snap to attention, salute the audience, then wave to them

Spit Hallo, folks!
Polish Hi, kids!
Spit Well, that's it. You can wake Granny up now, it's nearly time to go.
Polish (*sighing*) Ahh!

They encourage the audience to sigh, etc.

Spit Did you enjoy it?

Act II, Scene 5

"Yes!" from the audience

Polish Why, what were you doin'?

Patsy enters, waving to the audience

Eh?!!
Patsy Hallo! ... Hallo! ... Hallo!
Spit Look out! Here's [topical female personality]!
Polish [some derogatory remark to suit]!
Patsy Oy! There's no need to be rude! Just because I'm not royalty any more!
Spit Never mind. In our eyes you'll always be an old queen.
Patsy Oh, thanks ... (*She double-takes*) What!
Polish We were just saying goodbye to our mates out there.
Patsy That's why I'm 'ere. (*To the audience*) You can't go just yet. You've all got to give me a sample!
Spit
Polish } (*together*) Eh?!!
Patsy Of their singin' voices!
Spit
Polish } (*together*) Oh, yeah!
Patsy (*to the audience*) You thought you'd got away with it, didn't ya? (*To someone*) Don't worry, you'll still be in time for last orders, luv! (*To the duo*) Now, 'ave you got the lyrics?
Polish No, it's just the way we're standin'.
Patsy I mean the words of the song they're gonna sing!
Spit
Polish } (*together; calling to the side*) HORACE! HORACE!

Horace trots on to C. He has the song sheet hung over his back with the words obscured

Patsy Don't tell me! It's something from "Fiddler on the Hoof"!
Horace (*shaking head*) Neigh!
Patsy "The Horse of the Rising Sun"?
Horace (*shaking head*) Neigh!
Patsy "Singin' in the Mane"?
Horace (*shaking head*) Neigh!
Patsy Oh, I give up!

Horace turns to reveal the words of the song

Oh, goody! It's [name of chosen song]! (*To the audience*) You all know that one! Right! Let's 'ave some lights an' give it a try!

The House Lights come up

We'll 'elp you! (*To Conductor / Pianist*) Hand brake off, dear!

Song 17

They have fun getting the audience to sing along. Horace keeps turning around, obscuring the words, etc. If desired, Children can be brought up on to the stage to sing and meet Horace. They return to their seats, and the House Lights go down

Patsy, Spit and Polish and Horace run off stage, waving goodbye to the audience

The Lights fade to black-out

A fanfare sounds

Scene 6

The Grand Finale

The Lights come up on a special finale setting, or one of the full stage sets

Bright lighting and bouncy music, as everyone enters to take their bows. The last to enter are Humpty and Fiona, magnificently attired

Humpty	I, Humpty Dumpty sat on a wall.
Spit	We made Humpty have a great fall.
King	All my horses and all my men,
Polish	Couldn't put Humpty together again.
Queen	Humpty Dumpty was vile and vicious,
Penelope	He threatened us all with his magic wishes.
Good Fairy	But in the end he saw the light,
Captain	And everything has turned out right.
Fiona	He proved he had a better side.
Patsy	He really is his mother's pride!
Jinxit	Doesn't it make you want to spit!
	Double crossed by a half-pint twit!
Good Fairy	You must admit, my grumpy friend,
	That goodness triumphs in the end.
Patsy	And now it's time for us to go,
All	GOODBYE FROM HUMPTY AND HIS EGG!

Song 18

Finale song or reprise

FURNITURE AND PROPERTY LIST

Further dressing may be added at the director's discretion

ACT 1

Scene 1

On stage: Front-cloth showing weird, surreal landscape

Off stage: Enormous egg on trolley (**Fairies**)

Personal: **Jinxit**: magic wand
Good Fairy: magic wand (carried throughout)

During black-out on page 5

Strike: Enormous egg

Scene 2

On stage: Back-cloth showing seaside resort with beach and pier, etc.
On Patsy's B&B: hanging-baskets; window-boxes
On B&B front-door: hanging sign reading "EGG VIEW B&B".
    Underneath sign: smaller hanging sign reading "NO VACANCIES" with "VACANCIES" on reverse
Low wall with thicker section. *On thicker section*: enormous egg
    Below egg on wall: plaque reading "THE GIANT EGG OF EGG-TON-ON-SEA. DO NOT TOUCH."
Sign-post pointing off L reading "TO THE BEACH"
Seaside holiday paraphernalia (**Chorus**)

Off Stage: Suitcase (**Patsy**)
Rifles (**Spit and Polish**)
Piece of cake (**Humpty**)

Personal: **Jinxit**: peculiar-looking umbrella (Carried throughout)

During the black-out on page 21

Strike: Enormous egg

Set: Two enormous halves of broken eggshell

Scene 3

On stage: Front-cloth showing a pathway leading down to the sea and beach

Off stage: Bulging supermarket bag. *In it*: food for Humpty (**Patsy**)

Scene 4

On stage: Sea and sky backcloth
Ground rows of stylized waves, or alternative effect
Brightly painted beach hut
Larger beach hut bearing the royal crest, with curtained opening. *On it*: sign reading "KEEP OUT! NO RIFF-RAFF ALLOWED."
Tall rocks and sand dunes
Low sea rocks
Seaside paraphernalia including buckets and spades, sand-castles, beach balls, towels, ice-creams, etc.

Off stage: Large brassière (**Horace**)
Folded deckchair (**Patsy**)
Three ice-cream cones (**Fiona**)
Beach balls (**Chorus and Dancers**)
Large ice-creams in cone (**Humpty**)

Personal: **Patsy**: wad of banknotes

ACT II

Scene 1

On stage: Front-cloth showing a weird, surreal landscaoe

Scene 2

On stage: Canopied dais with steps. *On it*: two large golden thrones; scattered empty food cartons, sweet wrappers, empty drinks cans, etc.
Large slice of pizza (**Humpty**)
Open pizza-box (**Footman**)

Off Stage: Trays laden with mouth-watering food — roast meats, pies, huge iced-cakes, giant jellies, etc. (**Junior Cooks**)
Trays of chips (**Small Junior Cooks**)
Dustpan and brush (**Queen**)
Broom and small dustbin (**King**)
Small decorated cart. *On it*: motor horn (**Patsy, Spit, Polish** and **Horace**)
Comic number plate. i.e."Wide Load" (**Polish**)

Furniture and Property List

Personal: **Small Cook**: salt shaker under hat

Scene 3

On stage: Front-cloth showing grim stone walls, high barred window, manacles and chains, etc.
Rough bench

Scene 4

On stage: As ACT 1 Scene 2

Off Stage: Two halves of giant broken eggshell (**Patsy** and **Humpty**)

During black-out on page 74

Strike: Two halves of giant broken eggshell

Set: Enormous egg

Scene 5

On stage: Front-cloth as Act I, Scene 3

Off stage: Song sheet (**Horace**)

Scene 6

On stage: Special setting or one of the full stage sets can be used

LIGHTING PLOT

Practical fittings required: nil

Various interior and exterior settings

* Optional lighting cues

ACT I, Scene 1. Domain of the Bad Luck Fairy

To open: Sinister exterior lighting DS. Flashes of lightning

Cue 1	**Good Fairy** "Bring at once the egg to me!" *Bright and magical lighting*	(Page 3)
Cue 2	**Good Fairy** points her wand. Blinding flash *Black-out*	(Page 4)
Cue 3	**Humpty** exits in the black-out; when ready *Restore previous state*	(Page 4)
Cue 4	**Jinxit** raises her wand *Darken to sinister lighting*	(Page 4)
Cue 5	**Jinxit** points her wand. **Good Fairy**'s helpers giggle *Brighten lighting*	(Page 4)
Cue 6	**Jinxit** waves her wand over the egg. Blinding flash *Black-out*	(Page 5)
Cue 7	Enormous egg is struck in black-out; when ready *Bring up eerie spotlight on* **Jinxit**	(Page 5)
Cue 8	**Jinxit** exits *Fade spotlight to black-out*	(Page 5)

ACT I, Scene 2. Eggton-On-Sea. Many years later

To open: Full bright exterior lighting

Cue 9	**Patsy** waves and exits into the B&B *Darken to sinister lighting*	(Page 8)

Lighting Plot

Cue 10	**Jinxit** rushes over to the enormous egg *Bring up eerie follow-spot on* **Jinxit**	(Page 8)
Cue 11	**Jinxit** moves DR and lurks *Fade follow-spot. Bring up bright exterior lighting*	(Page 9)
Cue 12	**Jinxit** points her wand to the sky *Flash of lightning*	(Page 20)
Cue 13	Roll of thunder *Darken to sinister lighting*	(Page 20)
Cue 14	**Jinxit** points her wand at the sky *Flash of lightning*	(Page 21)
Cue 15	**Jinxit** points her wand at the sky a second time *Blinding flash of lightning*	(Page 21)
Cue 16	Tremendous clap of thunder *Black-out*	(Page 21)
Cue 17	Broken eggshell is set in black-out. When ready *Bring up general exterior lighting*	(Page 21)
Cue 18	**Humpty**: "... were my dotin' mother!" *Dim general exterior lighting*	(Page 25)
Cue 19	Everyone freezes, except **Patsy** and **Humpty** *Bring up rosy spotlight on* **Patsy**. *After short comic business and when ready cut spotlight and restore previous general exterior setting*	(Page 25)
Cue 20	**Humpty** strikes an arrogant pose. When ready *Fade lights to black-out*	(Page 26)

ACT I, SCENE 3. On the Way to the Beach

To open: General exterior lighting DS

Cue 21	**Junxit** enters DL *Dim lighting and bring up eerie follow-spot on* **Jinxit**	(Page 27)
Cue 22	**Jinxit** moves to DL and sulks *Fade out follow-spot and brighten general exterior lighting*	(Page 27)
Cue 23	**Patsy**: "Your mummy's comin'!" *Begin to fade lights*	(Page 31)

Cue 24	**Patsy** exits DL *Black-out*	(Page 31)

ACT 1, SCENE 4. The Beach at Eggton-On-Sea

To open: Full exterior lighting; bright blazing sunshine effect

Cue 25	**Captain**: "Moments like this." *Romantic lighting*	(Page 35)
Cue 26	At the end of **Song 7** *Restore previous lighting state*	(Page 35)
Cue 27	**Humpty**: " ... ruling king!!" Flash *Black-out*	(Page 40)
Cue 28	**Humpty** puts on the **King**'s crown; when ready *Restore previous lighting state*	(Page 40)

ACT II, SCENE 1. Domain of the Bad Luck Fairy

To open: Dark sinister lighting DS. Flash of lightning

Cue 29	The **Good Fairy** appears *Brighten lighting*	(Page 43)
Cue 30	The **Good Fairy** waves her wand. Flash *Black-out*	(Page 44)

ACT II, SCENE 2. The Royal Palace

To open: Full general interior lighting

Cue 31	At the end of **Song 13** (Reprise of 10) *Fade to black-out*	(Page 59)

ACT II, SCENE 3. A Dungeon Cell

To open: Very dark and gloomy interior lighting DS

Cue 32	**Jinxit** enters *Bring up eerie spotlight on **Jinxit** DL*	(Page 59)
Cue 33	**Jinxit** exits *Cut spotlight. Brighten interior lighting*	(Page 59)
Cue 34	To start Song 14 (optional) *Dim general lighting. Bring up follow-spots, etc.*	(Page 61)

Lighting Plot

*Cue 35	At end of **Song 14 (Optional)** *Cut follow-spots, etc*	(Page 62)
Cue 36	**Penelope**: "But who is she?" . Flash *Brighten interior lighting*	(Page 62)
Cue 37	The **Good Fairy** waves her wand *Fade lights to black-out*	(Page 63)

ACT II, SCENE 4. Eggton-On-Sea

To open: Full general bright exterior lighting

*Cue 38	**Jinxit, Humpty** and the **King's Men** exit. Music plays *Strobe lighting effect*	(Page 71)
*Cue 39	**Horace** exits *Cut strobe and restore previous state*	(Page 71)
Cue 40	**Humpty**: " That giant eggshell!" Flash *Black-out*	(Page 74)
Cue 41	Enormous egg is set. **Jinxit** exits. When ready *Bring up general exterior lighting with spotlight on enormous egg*	(Page 75)
Cue 42	The **Good Fairy** waves her wand. Flash *Black-out*	(Page 77)
Cue 43	The egg is struck. The **Good Fairy** and **Helpers** exit *Restore general exterior lighting*	(Page 78)

ACT II, SCENE 5. A Spot of Yolk Singing

To open: General exterior lighting

Cue 44	**Patsy**: " ... give it a try!" *Bring house lights up*	(Page 79)
Cue 45	At the end of Song 17 *Fade house lights*	(Page 80)
Cue 46	**Patsy, Spit and Polish,** and **Horace** exit *Fade to black-out*	(Page 80)

ACT II, SCENE 6. The Grand Finale

To open: Bright general lighting

No cues

EFFECTS PLOT

ACT I

Cue 1	To open ACT I *Unearthly sounds. Rolls of thunder*	(Page 1)
Cue 2	Spooky music. When ready *Flash* DL	(Page 1)
Cue 3	**Jinxit** and **Humpty** move towards the exit DL *Flash* DR	(Page 2)
Cue 4	The **Good Fairy** points her wand at **Humpty** *Blinding flash*	(Page 4)
Cue 5	**Jinxit** waves her wand over the egg *Flash*	(Page 5)
Cue 6	**Jinxit** makes magical gestures. Lightning flash *Roll of thunder*	(Page 20)
Cue 7	**Jinxit** points her wand at the sky. Lightning flash *Roll of thunder*	(Page 21)
Cue 8	**Jinxit** points her wand at the sky. Blinding lightning flash *Tremendous clap of thunder*	(Page 21)
Cue 10	Black-out *Sound of egg breaking and falling*	(Page 21)
Cue 11	**Humpty**: " ... ruling king!!" *Flash*	(Page 40)

ACT II

Cue 12	To open ACT II. Flash of lighting *Roll of thunder*	(Page 43)
Cue 13	**Jinxit**: "Ha! Ha! Ha!" *Flash* DR	(Page 43)

Effects Plot

Cue 14	The **Good Fairy** waves her wand *Flash*	(Page 44)
Cue 15	**Jinxit** exits. The lighting becomes brighter *Sound of heavy door creaking open* DR	(Page 59)
Cue 16	The **Queen, King, Captain** and **Penelope** enter *Sound of heavy door clanging shut* DR	(Page 59)
Cue 17	**Captain**: " Shh! Listen! What's that?" *Sound of heavy door creaking open* DR	(Page 61)
Cue 18	**Captain**: " ... come to let us out?" *Sound of heavy door clanging shut* DR	(Page 61)
Cue 19	**Penelope**: "But who is she?" *Flash*	(Page 62)
Cue 20	**Humpty**: " ...that giant eggshell!" *Flash*	(Page 74)
Cue 21	Magical music. Confused cries from the cast *Loud echoing scream from* **Jinxit,** *diminishing into silence*	(Page 74)
Cue 22	Noisy, heated argument amongst **Principals** and **Chorus** *Flash*	(Page 77)
Cue 23	The **Good Fairy** waves her wand over the egg *Flash*	(Page 77)

www.ingramcontent.com/pod-product-compliance
Lightning Source LLC
LaVergne TN
LVHW051750080426
835511LV00018B/3286